Physical Characteristics of the Bedlington Terrier

(from the The Kennel Club breed standard)

Body: Muscular and markedly flexible. Chest deep and fairly broad. Flat ribbed, deep through brisket which reaches to elbow. Back has natural arch over loin creating a definite tuck-up of underline. Body slightly greater in length than height.

Tail: Moderate length, thick at root, tapering to a point and gracefully curved. Set-on low.

Coat: Very distinctive. Thick and linty, standing well out from skin, but not wiry. A distinct tendency to twist, particularly on head and face.

Hindquarters: Muscular and moderate length, arched loin with curved topline immediately above loins. Hindlegs have appearance of being longer than forelegs. Hocks strong and well let down, turning neither in nor out.

Size: About 41 cms (16 ins) at withers. This allows for slight variation below in the case of a bitch and above in the case of a dog.

Weight: 8–10 kgs (18–23 lbs).

Feet: Long harefeet with thick and well closed up pads.

Bedlington Terrier

By Muriel P Lee

Unearth the fascinating origins of the Bedlington Terrier, originally called the Rothbury Terrier of the Border Counties, as a 'gypsy dog' to miners and tinkers, to a hard-as-nails ratter and fighter, to its modern-day role as a companion and show dog in Britain, the USA and beyond.

Find out what lies beneath the Bedlighton Terrier's lamb-like appearance and you will discover a talented, versatile and athletic canine companion, whose diminutive size and 'woolly' resemblance are somewhat deceiving. The Bedlington is no softie, but rather a hard-working, instinctive terrier who can earn his keep, protect the children or entertain the household, as the task demands.

Learn the requirements of a well-bred Bedlington Terrier by studying the description of the breed as set forth in The Kennel Club's breed standard. Both show dogs and pets must possess key characteristics as outlined in the breed standard.

Be advised about choosing a reputable breeder and selecting a healthy, typical puppy. Understand the responsibilities of ownership, including home preparation, acclimatisation, the vet and prevention of common puppy problems.

Enter into a sensible discussion of dietary and feeding considerations, exercise, grooming, travelling and identification of your dog. This chapter discusses Bedlington Terrier care for all stages of development.

CONTENTS

PUBLISHED IN THE UNITED KINGDOM BY:

INTERPET
PUBLISHING
Vincent Lane, Dorking, Surrey RH4 3YX England

ISBN 1-903098-85-8

PHOTOGRAPHS BY DAVID DALTON, ISABELLE FRANÇAIS,
CAROL ANN JOHNSON, ALICE VAN KEMPEN, KAREN TAYLOR,
MICHAEL TRAFFORD AND LARA STERN
with additional photos by Norvia Behling, TJ Calhoun, Carolina Biological Supply, Doskocil, James Hayden-Yoav, James R Hayden, RBP, Bill Jonas, Dwight R Kuhn, Dr Dennis Kunkel, Mikki Pet Products, Phototake, Jean Claude Revy and Dr Andrew Spielman.
Illustrations by Renée Low

The publisher wishes to thank Valerie Armstead, Ronnie Armstead-Williams, Shirley Davies, Mary Jo Dunn, Linda Freeman, Candace Sandfort, Peggy M Schulman and the rest of the owners for allowing their dogs to be photographed for this book.

The Bedlington Terrier has become known world-wide for its distinct appearance. While beautiful and dainty-looking, the Bedlington is both hardy and agile—a true terrier in 'lamb's' clothes!

Have you ever seen a dog being walked on the street by his master and thought, 'What is that? It looks like a lamb!' That adorable 'lambkin' is the Bedlington Terrier. Although he may look like a lamb, this is a dog that is all terrier, one who has the heart of a lion but is a charming, gentle and first-class companion. Although he is most often now a loyal companion for his family, his original terrier instincts have not been lost. He will be equally at home on a country estate chasing a rabbit or in a London flat lounging about with his owner.

The Bedlington Terrier may not be the dog for everyone, as terriers are active, busy dogs and this dog is no exception. However, if you like a plucky dog, one who fits easily into most any lifestyle, this may be just the one for you.

WHAT IS A TERRIER?
As with that of all terriers, the history of the Bedlington Terrier is a convoluted and difficult road to follow. Edwin Brough wrote in the early 1900s, 'He who attempts to discover the origin and trace the history of any one of our breeds of dogs, beyond a compara-

GENUS *CANIS*

Dogs and wolves are members of the genus *Canis*. Wolves are known scientifically as *Canis lupus* while dogs are known as *Canis domesticus*. Dogs and wolves are known to interbreed. The term *canine* derives from the Latin derived word *Canis*. The term *dog* has no scientific basis but has been used for thousands of years. The origin of the word 'dog' has never been authoritatively ascertained.

tively few generations, will, in most or all cases, speedily find himself in a fog, tossed on a sea of doubt, driven hither and thither by the conflicting evidence of the writers he consults, who seem to emulate each other in the meagreness of the information they give and the vagueness with which they convey it.'

Hoping to defy any sense of the meagre and vague, let us begin. The Bedlington Terrier belongs to the classification of dogs described as terriers, from the Latin word *terra*, meaning earth. The terrier is a dog that has been bred to work beneath the ground to drive out small and large vermin, rodents and other animals that can be a nuisance to country living. Nearly all of the dogs in the Terrier Group originated in the British Isles with the exception of the Australian Terrier, the Cesky Terrier and the American Staffordshire Terrier. Although these breeds do not hail from the British Isles, they were developed from British dogs: the Cesky Terrier from an original cross of the Scottish Terrier and the Sealyham Terrier, the Australian Terrier from a series of crosses of various terrier breeds and the American Staffordshire Terrier from the Staffordshire Bull Terrier.

Many of the terrier breeds were derived from a similar ancestor and, as recently as the mid-1800s, the terriers fell roughly into two basic categories: the rough-coated, short-legged dogs, which tended to come from Scotland, and the longer legged, smooth-coated dogs, which were bred in England. The terriers, although they may differ in type, all have the same character, being game dogs who go to ground after vermin or larger animals.

In 1735, the *Sportsman's Dictionary* described the terrier as a kind of hound, used only or chiefly for hunting the fox or badger. 'He creeps into the ground and then nips and bites the fox and badger, either by tearing them in pieces with his teeth, or else hauling them and pulling them by force out of their lurking holes.'

The terrier background is obscure, but what is certain is that in the 1700s and early 1800s there was no definite breed of terrier, but dogs that were bred to go to ground with courage and conviction. Those who were unable to do the job were destroyed, and those who could do the proper work were bred to one another with little regard for type. 'Unless they were fit and game for the purpose, their heads were not kept long out of the huge butt of water in the stable yard.'

Those who bred and kept dogs had a specific purpose of work for their particular breed—long legs for speed, short legs for going to ground and double coats for protection against the elements. Regardless of their intended quarry, all terriers have a powerful set of teeth.

ORIGIN OF THE BEDLINGTON TERRIER

Originally called the Rothbury Terrier, the Bedlington hails from the Border Counties between

England and Scotland. This is rocky, hilly country where there is an abundance of wildlife and vermin—ideal terrier country! Also from this area are the Border Terrier, the Dandie Dinmont Terrier and the Lakeland Terrier. They are all keenly game and natural hunters that have courage and stamina and are able to go to ground after rats, rabbits, foxes,

In the 1930s, Mr John Cornforth's Nelson was typical of the Bedlingtons of that period—a marked difference from the dogs of today.

A very famous champion at the end of the nineteenth century was Ch Humbleden Blue Boy. Note that the trimming of that time is quite different from that of today. The head shows a stop, which is not apparent in present-day dogs.

badgers, otters and martens.

Although the Bedlington's background is vague, there are some general assumptions that can be made as far as the Bedlington's roots are concerned. It is assumed that one of the foundation dogs is the Old English Terrier, with crosses to the Otterhound and possibly to the Dandie Dinmont. On occasion, it has been mentioned that the Whippet is also in the Bedlington's background because of the similarity in conformation, including the dog's head shape and abdominal tuck-up, and the Bedlington's speed, but, in general, this is refuted by most experts.

A dog by the name of Old Flint, whelped in 1782, is considered to be the progenitor of the modern breed. In the early 1820s, Joseph Aynsley from the town of Bedlington in Northhampshire, purchased Peachem and bred him to Phoebe, and they produced a son named Piper. Aynsley then acquired a bitch called Cotes Phoebe, who was bred to Anderson's Piper. Thus, the breed had its start.

In 1873 the first Stud Book of The Kennel Club listed 30 Bedlingtons, but noted that the majority of them were listed as 'Pedigree not recorded,' 'Unknown' or 'Uncertain,' and only 11 had the names of their sires and dams recorded.

Around the early 1900s, not only were better records being kept, but the breed started to be bred as a companion dog and, surprisingly, became a dog who had manners and a taste for luxury. Methods of trimming improved and the dog took on the look of a lovely sheared lamb; however, the heart of a terrier still beat and the Bedlington has never lost its terrier skills of going after game and vermin.

The first dog show with a class for Bedlingtons was held at Newcastle in 1879, with an entry of 52. Mr Pickett, who was an ardent supporter of the breed, won with his dog Tear 'em. In 1871 Mr Pickett again won the breed over an entry of 22 with a bitch called Tyneside. At the 1873 show Pickett won first place with the bitch Tyne, a sister to Tear

A delightful photo showing the young Master Horlick with two of his family's favourite Bedlingtons.

'em. Tear 'em placed second and Tyneside was third. Pickett said that no breed could compare with the Bedlington for stamina, courage and resolution.

Pickett wrote, 'I look upon the Bedlington as a farmer's friend and country gentleman's companion. No breed of Terrier can compare with him for stamina, fire, courage and resolution. He will knock about all day with his master, busy as a bee at foxes, rabbits or otters; and at night, when any other sort of dog would be stiff, sore and utterly jaded, he will turn up bright as a new shilling and ready for any game going. He takes to the water readily, has a capital nose, is most intelligent and lively and is a rough and ready friend about the fields and woods—he has no equal.'

Miss Lawis, owner of a Bedlington kennel, shown arriving at the 1934 Crufts Show. The dog on the left won a Challenge Certificate.

Mrs Maud Mead, Sudston Kennels, purchased a dog named Raggles in 1909 from his breeder, E Hurley, and remained a supporter, fancier and breeder up until the mid-1930s. She devoted her efforts to the British Bedlington Club, formed in 1910 by Percy Smith. By 1933, however, many of its members had left the club to join the more successful Bedlington Terrier Association, which had been established in 1924.

Bet of Bransways being trimmed by Miss Branfoot.

By 1934, the British Bedlington Club had disbanded due to declining membership. The Sudston Cup, named after Mrs Mead's kennel, was then transferred to the National Bedlington Terrier Club. Her Sudston Panther was a well-known sire of the area, described by his breeder as 'A fine upstanding dog, on the large side, but entirely free from coarseness. An enormously long, fine head, flat, well-placed ears, well-set eyes. Perfect front and grand outline.' The doggy press critic noted, 'Shade big but a wonderful bodied, boned and quartered dog; his blue coat handles well, and he has a long, shapely head; a most likely sire.'

THE BEDLINGTON IN THE USA
The Bedlington Terrier was exported to the United States in the late 1800s and the first entry to appear in the American Kennel

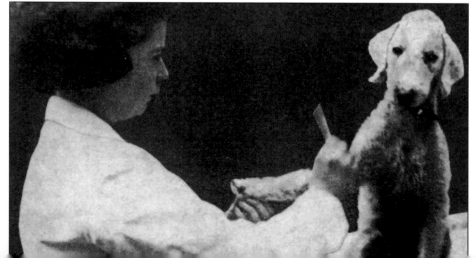

Miss Goodrick, an exhibitor of Bedlingtons during the 1930s, combing out a dog's legs before their appearance in the ring.

The look of the fully groomed modern American Bedlington Terrier.

Club Stud Book was in 1883. The breed was not a particularly popular dog in America and it took until 1924 for registrations to reach ten per year. However, the breed was somewhat more popular in Canada, where two litters were bred as early as 1883.

The first American championship won by a Bedlington was in 1884 by Ch Blucher, whelped in England in 1882. By the mid-1880s, a group of fanciers noted that the breed should be taken seriously and wrote the first American standard for the Bedlington. By 1900, there were five American champions of title, and 70 or so Bedlingtons had been registered. The going price of a pet puppy was $50.00, whereas a show prospect could cost the fantastic sum (for those times) of $500.00.

The Bedlington Terrier in America has been very fortunate, for over the years the breed was supported by several wealthy individuals and, through their efforts, the breed remained in the public eye for many years with exceptional winners coming from their kennels. During this period, from about 1920 through the mid-1960s, many exceptional Bedlingtons were whelped and shown in America, compiling wonderful winning records in addition to becoming top producers.

In the early 1900s the breed caught the eye of Col. M Robert Guggenheim and his Firenze Kennels in Long Island, New York. A dog man for years, the Colonel had owned over 60 Bulldogs at one time, in addition to a pack of 30 Beagles. He saw the Bedlington Terrier in England around 1905 and eventually imported the best of the Bedlingtons that he could find. Guggenheim had a top kennel man, the Englishman Edward Ward, who travelled the Atlantic on a yearly basis, keeping up on the English Bedlington news and bringing back the best of the breed to Firenze Kennels. Between 1920 and 1930, 29 Bedlington champions were made up in America, 23 of which were owned by Firenze Kennels.

GYPSY DOG?

Eugene Noble wrote in his article on 'The Gypsy Dogs,' 'His devotees were a rough set of hardy workingmen, miners, nailers, gypsies and tinkers, for the most part. They wanted something scrappy; a dog that would do or die; a lithe, agile, fearless gamester...Rough men, poor men, clever and canny men, fancied and bred the Bedlington.' Some believe that the tassel at the end of the Bedlington's ears is reminiscent of his past with the gypsies and their fancy earrings.

A well-groomed Bedlington Terrier who hails from the Netherlands.

This trend of importing English greats came to an end within a couple of decades. By 1940, nearly half of the US champions were either bred in America or Canada, whereas prior to this time, 80% of the champions had been imported from England.

Anthony and Anna Neary emigrated from England to the United States in 1929, bringing with them a pair of Bedlingtons called Exiled Laddie and Hasty Morn. 'Laddie' became an American champion and sired six champions. The Nearys were strong supporters of the breed, supporting major Bedlington entries at the Eastern shows. In 1940 they entered the very prestigious Westminster Kennel Club show and their dog was selected Best American-bred Terrier. William Rockefeller was at this show and later called the Nearys, offering Mr Neary the position of kennel manager of his Rock Ridge Kennels.

The Rockefellers and the Nearys proved to be an unbeatable combination in the US. Numerous champions came out of this kennel for over three decades, up until Mr Neary's retirement from kennel managing and handling. The outstanding dog from the Rock Ridge Kennels was Ch Rock Ridge Night Rocket, whelped in 1946. For the time, he had one of the top show careers of any dog of any breed. At little more than one year of age, he was Best in Show at the prestigious Morris and Essex show, the show held on the grounds of the estate of Mrs Geraldine Dodge. The next February, he was Best in Show at Westminster Kennel Club and, the following year, he again was Best at the Morris and Essex show. He was used sparingly at stud but in a short and limited career he sired 36 champions. To this day, he remains one of the greats among Bedlington Terriers.

Another American kennel of renown, started in the mid-1930s, was Rowanoaks Kennels, owned by Col. and Mrs P V G Mitchell and their daughter, Connie Willemsen. The Mitchells travelled to England and imported two outstanding dogs: Ch Tarragona of Rowanoaks and Ch Love Letter. Tarragona went to the top in the show ring, in addition to siring 23 champions. However, within a year, his daughter, Ch Lady Rowena of Rowanoaks, bested him in the ring, winning an all-breed Best in Show in 1938 while still in the Puppy Class. In 1939 she won Best in Show at the well-known American terrier show, Montgomery County Kennel Club.

The Mitchells, very active in the breed for many years, bred for correct breed type, beautiful heads and proper coats. They never kept more than 12 dogs and finished

BRAIN AND BRAWN

Since dogs have been inbred for centuries, their physical and mental characteristics are constantly being changed to suit man's desires for hunting, retrieving, scenting, guarding and warming their masters' laps. During the past 150 years, dogs have been judged according to physical characteristics as well as functional abilities. Few breeds can boast a genuine balance between physique, working ability and temperament.

over 100 champions. They were active until the late 1960s and their daughter, Mrs Willemsen, was also very active in the Bedlington Terrier Club of America.

In America, by the 1950s and 1960s, many new breeders became active, producing more notable dogs. Martha McVay of Marvay Kennels in California has been active for nearly half a century. Dogs from her kennel have placed in many Groups through the years, in addition to winning the national speciality for six years.

Milo and Marjorie Hanson from California and their Valgo Kennels produced over 75 champions and also earned obedience degrees on several more. Center Ridge Kennels in Milwaukee, Wisconsin, finished

30 champions. Ch Center Ridge Snow Classic, whelped in 1955, won 5 Bests in Show and 40 Group firsts. Am and Can Ch Center Ridge Minute Man had two Bests in Show and sired nine champion get. Am and Can Ch Center Ridge Lady Caroline, whelped in 1959, won 15 Bests in Show and 62 Group firsts, and still had time to produce 2 champion get.

In 1948, 218 Bedlingtons were registered in the US and, by 1958, registrations had more than doubled to 573. By 1968, registrations had risen to 778.

Mrs Marian Cabage from Illinois was active in the 1960s and her most well-known dog was Ch Southwind's Blue Velvet, the top terrier in 1969 and also recipient of the *Kennel Review* Award for that year. He retired with 18 Bests in Show and 125 Group firsts, and having sired 32 champions.

David Ramsey of Willow Wind Kennels was the Bedlington breeder who made the greatest impact on the breed during the last quarter of the 20th century. Ch Willow Wind Silver Cloud, sire of 15 champions, was the top Bedlington sire in 1980. His double-granddaughter was the top Bedlington in 1983. Mr Ramsey's greatest dog was Ch Willow Wind Centurian. At the Beverly Hills show, Centurian defeated 700 terriers to win the Terrier Group.

In the 1990s, Ch Willow Wind Play It My Way was a multi-Best in Show dog. Ch Willow Wind Tenure was the top terrier in 1999.

In America the Bedlington has remained fairly popular. The breed has been fortunate to have some exceptional owners over the years who have been interested in having their dogs campaigned; these dogs have made the breed memorable, even though the breed's numbers and popularity have been fairly small. In the late 1990s the breed was 124th in popularity out of 146 breeds, and there were 177 registrations.

THE BEDLINGTON IN BRITAIN
Returning to England, the Rathsrigg Kennel of Ian and Margaret Phillips, West Yorkshire, was established in 1957. Mr Phillips has certainly been a force in the breed in the UK. Over the years, they have bred about 25 English champions in addition to selling dogs throughout Europe, Scandinavia and North America. Mr Phillips is president of the National Bedlington Terrier Club and has written a extensive book, *The Centenary Book of the National Bedlington Terrier Club, 1989-1998*, which is available from either Mr Phillips or from the club.

Notable British breeders have included Mrs P Hall of Dalip Bedlingtons. She bred and co-owned, with Mrs P Morton, Ch Dalip Lord of the Rings, who was the top Bedlington and the top sire of 2000, winning a total of 19 Challenge Certificates and 14 Bests of Breed, in addition to winning two Terrier Groups by the end of 2000.

Mr and Mrs R North own Niddvale Spring Warrier, the Best of Breed winner at Crufts in 2000. Toffset Tiptop, owned by Mr and Mrs Wright, won the bitch CC and Best of Breed at the 2000 Welsh Kennel Club show. Mrs B F Emsley owned Ch Hilldyke Alicia, who was Best of Breed at the National Terrier show and top Bedlington bitch in 2000. Mrs Emsley is secretary/treasurer of the National Bedlington Terrier Club, which publishes the very informative *The Sporting Bedlington*, published twice a year.

At the 2000 Crufts Dog Show, 80 Bedlington Terriers were entered, which placed the breed numerically about in the middle of terrier entries, but far below the more popular terrier breeds.

BEDLINGTONS AROUND THE WORLD
In Canada the Bedlington Terrier has remained somewhat of an uncommon breed, and its fanciers usually show their dogs in both Canada and the United States. Well-known breeders since the 1960s have been Shirley and Don

A group of handsone Bedlingtons with their mistresses.

Martin of the Siwash Kennels in Ontario, and the Boulevardier Kennels of M Gail Gates and Art Perkins from Saskatchewan. From the Siwash Kennels, all dogs owner-handled, came numerous top winners. Ch Siwash Blue Kelley was second top terrier in 1983 and third top terrier in 1984, won 3 Bests in Show and 27 Group firsts and was Best of Opposite Sex at Montgomery County Kennel Club in 1990 at the age of nine. Ch Marvay's Melissa of Siwash was the number-four terrier in 1978 and had three all-breed Bests in Show. Ch Siwash Merry Martin was the number-one Bedlington in Canada in 1989, with multiple Group placements. In 1988, *Dogs in Canada* listed the top five dogs in each breed for the previous 25 years, and four of the five

Bedlingtons were from the Siwash Kennel.

Boulevardier Bedlingtons, since 1987, have held the number-one Bedlington in Canada position for four different years with four different dogs. Ch Boulevardier SeltineTiere was number-three Bedlington in 1994 and number-two Bedlington in 1995, as well as number-eight Bedlington in the USA. Ch Boulevardier Bad LeRoy Brown, owned by Elmer Grieve, was number-one Bedlington in 1994. Ch Trout on a Line finished his championship with four consecutive Group placements. The motto for this kennel is, 'In search of excellence in conformation, temperament and health equally important.'

Angela Roper of Nosehill Kennels, of Alberta, should also

A well-balanced and well-groomed young Bedlington Terrier.

winner at the Helsinki International show in 1964. Int Ch Jessica, bred by Mr Ilpo Malmioja, was best terrier in 1975. Ms Ritva Kohijoki of Kisapirtin Kennels has been well-known for her great winners; of note are Int Ch Kisapirtin Perro, Int Ch Kisapirtin Miramari, Int Ch Kisapirtin Talita and Int Kisapirtin Perella. Over the years she has had 12 International Championships, 37 Finnish Championships and about 120 CACIBs. There were approximately 175 Bedlingtons in Finland in the 1990s, and the breed is able to hold its own at the shows.

The breed is not very popular in New Zealand and by far the most active breeder is Linda Strongman, who purchased Aust and NZ Ch Southridge Royal Blue. This dog had won several Australian Bests in Show before being exported to New Zealand, where he has been a Group winner as well as Reserve Best in Show several times. Ms Strongman has imported several more dogs from Australia and bred NZ Ch Lynmar Truffels, who has won many awards in New Zealand.

be mentioned. Her Ch Lady Alexander of Nosehill was Best in Show at the Alberta Kennel Club in 1989. Ms Roper has been active in obedience, pet therapy and agility training.

In Finland there has been interest in the breed since the 1960s, with some fine kennels breeding and importing winning dogs. Peggen, Hjordie and Erkki Tenlenius of Eho Kennels have been well-known for many years, especially for Int Ch Leasowes Damask Rose, Best in Show

BREED CLUBS

There are two very active clubs for the Bedlington Terrier. In the United Kingdom it is the National Bedlington Terrier Club, and in the USA it is the Bedlington

Terrier Club of America. In America there are two affiliate clubs, the Bedlington Terrier Club of Greater Chicago and the Bedlington Terrier Club of the West. For information on either national club, The Kennel Club or the American Kennel Club should be contacted for the current corresponding secretary's name and address. For further information on British breeders, the National Bedlington Terrier Club should be contacted.

The UK has one of the world's most active Bedlington Terrier breed clubs. Here, a Bedlington is exhibited at an outdoor show in England.

Characteristics of the
BEDLINGTON TERRIER

PERSONALITY

The Bedlington Terrier is a versatile dog and a great house dog and companion. If you like to work with your dog, you will find this breed to be a happy and willing participant in whatever area you choose, be it obedience work, agility, therapy, flyball and, of course, best of all, going-to-ground activities. This is a smart dog that likes to please, to keep busy and to be challenged. Give him any job that requires a bit of brain activity on his part and he will be absolutely delighted. Of course, because of his intelligence, it is best to establish very early on who is the head of the household and the very basic in obedience lessons is always a good idea.

The Bedlington is a well-beloved family dog, giving much and asking little in return. He likes to have appropriate attention

The Bedlington is an active, hardy, long-lived companion who can make himself at home almost anywhere. This veteran is still 'sitting pretty' at 12 years of age.

from the family and in return will give of himself and be a loving, contributing member of the family. He will be extremely loyal and is very good with children. However, in spite of his lamb-like appearance and soft looks, this is an athletic breed that is every inch a terrier. This is not a breed that will while away the hours quietly on your lap; rather, he will be curious and enthusiastic. He loves to play and entertain, and he will be a great companion dog. He is a good watchdog but is not a noisy breed, barking only when strangers come to the house. He is lively and inquisitive, and you will find him a delight to have with you.

Given his small size, he is a good city dog who not only remains quiet but also requires little space in a flat. Unlike many dogs, he does not shed, but he does require weekly coat care.

If you are a first-time dog owner, you must be aware of your responsibility toward your new friend—either keep your dog on a leash or in your fenced garden. Your Bedlington, if loose and trotting along at your side, might spot a squirrel across a busy street. His killer terrier instincts will react quickly and, oblivious to the traffic, he will dart across the street. Therefore, some rudimentary obedience training should be in line so your pal will sit when asked to, come when

PART OF THE FAMILY
Bedlington Terriers thrive in organised activities and love to be a part of the family—going for rides in the car, fetching a ball, helping in the kitchen by keeping the floor clean and then cuddling up on the bed when day is done.

called and, in general, act like a gentleman.

Bedlingtons, as with other terriers, can be a challenge in the obedience ring. Terriers are not easy breeds to work with in obedience, as with their intelligence and independent spirit, they can sometimes be more trying to train than had been anticipated. You will see Golden Retrievers, Poodles and Miniature Schnauzers in abundance in obedience classes, as these are breeds with which it is easier to work. Not only are these breeds intelligent but, more importantly, they have a willingness to please their masters, a trait that is not

found in abundance in the terrier breeds.

    The terrier is easily distracted and busy, but he is an intelligent dog and he does respond to training. Of course, when training a smart and independent dog, the handler will often learn humility while the dog is learning his sits and stays. The Bedlington is a quick, alert and smart little dog who likes his owner to be his equal.

COAT CARE REQUIREMENTS
The Bedlington Terrier is a dog that will require weekly grooming, whether you are going to show the dog or just have him as a pet. If you are going to show your dog, be sure to buy your puppy from a reputable breeder who also shows

LIVING WITH A TERRIER
Brian Commons wrote, 'Terriers, created to hunt down and kill vermin, should all be sold with their own leather jackets. They are often feisty, lively, self-assured. You live with terriers, you do not own them'

his animals. He will be able to show you how to clip your dog into the proper show trim and he will also assist you with the finer points of grooming this breed.

If you are buying your Bedlington to be a pet, you will be able to do the trimming yourself (or have the dog professionally groomed) and, as time goes on, you will become as good a

Playful, intelligent and curious, the Bedlington wants nothing more than to be part of his owner's life.

DO YOU WANT TO LIVE LONGER?

If you like to volunteer, it is wonderful if you can take your dog to a nursing home once a week for several hours. The elder community loves to have a dog with which to visit, and often your dog will bring a bit of companionship to someone who is lonely or somewhat detached from the world. You will be not only bringing happiness to someone else but also keeping your dog busy—and we haven't even mentioned the fact that it has been discovered that volunteering helps to increase your own longevity!

HEART HEALTHY

The *Australian Medical Journal* in 1992 found that having pets is heart-healthy. Pet owners had lower blood pressure and lower levels of triglycerides than those who didn't have pets. It has also been found that senior citizens who own pets are more active and less likely to experience depression than those without pets.

Part of the pleasure of owning a Bedlington is pampering it with attentive grooming. Starting when your puppy is young will help him become accustomed to grooming and will give you lots of time to practise.

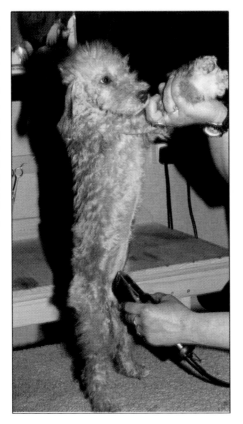

company. However, it will require some effort to do this.

The Bedlington has a non-shedding coat, which does require the removal of dead hair. Left untended, the coat will become matted and eventually smelly, and your dear pet will not be so nice to be around! A weekly or twice-weekly combing will take out the dead hair, making it unlikely that your Bedlington will develop a matted coat. Trimming, whether you have a show dog or a pet, will be required, but you will find it a fairly easy job to keep your dog in a pet trim.

HEALTH CONSIDERATIONS

By and large, Bedlington Terriers are very healthy dogs, as are most other terriers, and there are few health problems in the breed. Your only reliable option is to buy your puppy from a reputable breeder and ask the breeder if he has any health problems in his line. When buying a Bedlington Terrier, however, you must be aware that there is one significant health problem in the breed. You must ask the breeder of your dog if he is aware of the problem and has had his dogs tested.

This problem is copper toxicosis, which is a serious disease found in some Bedlington Terriers. This is an autosomal recessive disorder of copper accumulation that results in severe liver disease. It is an

groomer of the breed as a professional dog groomer! There are several books on grooming dogs in general, and both of the national breed clubs have grooming manuals for sale.

Do understand before purchasing your Bedlington Terrier that this is a breed with a coat that needs maintenance, whether you have a dog for the show ring or one that is a household pet. Keep your dog cleaned and trimmed, and you will find it a pleasure to be in his hereditary condition and one that cannot be ignored. At the present time, considerable research and study, both in England and in the United States, are being conducted. When buying your puppy, be sure to ask the breeder to see the biopsied 'normal' certificates of both the sire and dam. All responsible Bedlington breeders will have their dogs certified 'normal' before breeding them. It is thought that the disease may be present in as much as 50% of the breed; however, there was a time when two-thirds of the breed was affected. If your dog is biopsied as having the disease, there are now several therapies whereby the dog can be treated and often live a long and full life.

Although this health problem may look daunting, Bedlingtons are considered to be a very healthy breed. The problem mentioned exists in the breed, and a buyer should be aware of it. Do not be turned away from the breed, but do realise that if the breeder of your puppy is reputable and aware, he will be doing his utmost to breed healthy dogs.

This is what a properly groomed Bedlington in show trim should look like. A dog kept in pet trim will require regular grooming as well, though it will not be as extensive.

Breed Standard for the
BEDLINGTON TERRIER

As breeders started exhibiting at dog shows, it was realised that there must be more uniformity within each breed, i.e. all puppies in a litter should look alike as well as being of the same type as their sire and dam. Each breed approved by The Kennel Club has a standard that gives the reader a mental picture of what the specific breed should look like.

All reputable breeders strive to produce animals that will meet the requirements of the standard.

Many breeds were developed for a specific purpose, i.e. hunting, retrieving, going to ground, coursing, guarding, herding, etc. The terriers were all bred to go to ground and to pursue vermin. In addition to having a dog that looks like a

The breed's desired conformation, as set forth in the standard, is illustrated beautifully by this fine champion.

LATHY AND LINTY

In the Bedlington lexicon, 'lathy' means hard and muscular, supple and tough, but not stiff or inactive. The flat ribs give the elbows freedom of movement. 'Linty' refers to a particular feature of the coat that only the Bedlington has. The coat is not harsh and it is not soft. It forms a pile that stands out from the skin and, although it is twisty, it is never curly and has a spring to its texture.

proper Bedlington Terrier, the standard assures that he will have the personality, disposition and intelligence that are sought after in the breed. Standards were originally written by fanciers who had a love and a concern for the breed. They knew that the essential characteristics of the Bedlington Terrier were unlike those of any other breed and that care must be taken that these characteristics were maintained through the generations.

As time progressed and breeders became more aware that certain points of the dog needed a better description or more definition, breeders would meet together and work out a new standard. However, standards for any breed are never changed on a whim, and serious study and exchange between breeders take place before any move is made.

THE IDEAL SPECIMEN

According to The Kennel Club, 'The Breed Standard is the "Blueprint" of the ideal specimen in each breed approved by a governing body, e.g. The Kennel Club, the Fédération Cynologique Internationale (FCI) and the American Kennel Club.

'The Kennel Club writes and revises Breed Standards taking account of the advice of Breed Councils/Clubs. Breed Standards are not changed lightly to avoid "changing the standard to fit the current dogs" and the health and well-being of future dogs is always taken into account when new standards are prepared or existing ones altered.'

BREEDER'S BLUEPRINT

If you are considering breeding your bitch, it is very important that you are familiar with the breed standard. Reputable breeders breed with the intention of producing dogs that are as close as possible to the standard and that contribute to the advancement of the breed. Study the standard for both physical appearance and temperament, and make certain your bitch and your chosen stud dog measure up.

THE KENNEL CLUB BREED STANDARD FOR THE BEDLINGTON TERRIER

General Appearance: A graceful, lithe, muscular dog, with no signs of either weakness or coarseness. Whole head pear or wedge-shaped, and expression in repose mild and gentle.

Characteristics: Spirited and game, full of confidence. An intelligent companion with strong sporting instincts.

Temperament: Good-tempered, having an affectionate nature, dignified, not shy or nervous. Mild in repose but full of courage when roused.

Head and Skull: Skull narrow, but deep and rounded; covered with profuse silky 'top-knot' which should be nearly white. Jaws long and tapering. There must be no 'stop,' the line from occiput to nose end straight and unbroken. Well filled up beneath eye, close fitting lips, without flew. Nostrils large and well defined.

Eyes: Small, bright and deep-set. Ideal eye has appearance of being triangular. Blues a dark eye, blue and tans have lighter eye with amber lights, livers and sandies a light hazel eye.

Ears: Moderately sized, filbert-shaped, set-on low, and hanging flat to cheek. Thin and velvety in texture, covered with short fine hair with fringe of whitish silky hair at tip.

Mouth: Teeth large and strong. Scissor bite, i.e. upper teeth closely overlapping lower teeth and set square to the jaws.

Neck: Long and tapering, deep base with no tendency to throatiness. Springs well up from shoulders, and head carried rather high.

Forequarters: Forelegs straight, wider apart at chest than at feet. Pasterns long and slightly sloping without weakness. Shoulder flat and sloping.

Body: Muscular and markedly flexible. Chest deep and fairly broad. Flat ribbed, deep through brisket which reaches to elbow. Back has natural arch over loin creating a definite tuck-up of

BREEDING CONSIDERATIONS
The decision to breed your dog is one that must be considered carefully and researched thoroughly before moving into action. Some people believe that breeding will make their bitches happier or that it is an easy way to make money. Unfortunately, indiscriminate breeding only worsens the rampant problem of pet overpopulation, as well as putting a considerable dent in your pocketbook. As for the bitch, the entire process from mating through whelping is not an easy one and puts your pet under considerable stress. Last, but not least, consider whether or not you have the means to care for an entire litter of pups. Without a reputation in the field, your attempts to sell the pups may be unsuccessful.

Head study of a champion Bedlington, showing both proper structure and proper grooming.

Correct body structure, showing both grace and musculature with proper proportions.

Incorrect body structure; back is flat without natural arch over loin.

Correct forequarters; legs straight and strong, wider apart at chest than at feet.

Incorrect forequarters; wider at feet than at chest and toeing out.

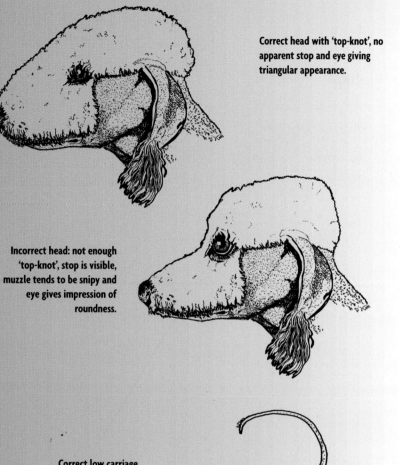

Correct head with 'top-knot', no apparent stop and eye giving triangular appearance.

Incorrect head: not enough 'top-knot', stop is visible, muzzle tends to be snipy and eye gives impression of roundness.

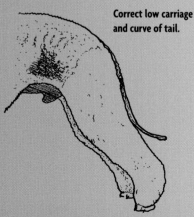

Correct low carriage and curve of tail.

Incorrect tail carriage; should not curve over back.

DID YOU KNOW?
Bedlington puppies are born either black, dark brown or chocolate and will turn to their adult colour by one year of age. The English standard gives the colours of the breed as blue, liver or sandy with or without tan. The American standard phrases the colours thusly: blue, sandy, liver, blue and tan, sandy and tan, and liver and tan.

Gait/Movement: Capable of galloping at high speed and have appearance of being able to do so. Action very distinctive, rather mincing, light and springy in slower paces and slight roll when in full stride.

Coat: Very distinctive. Thick and linty, standing well out from skin, but not wiry. A distinct tendency to twist, particularly on head and face.

Colour: Blue, liver or sandy with or without tan. Darker pigment to be encouraged. Blues and blue and tans must have black noses; livers and sandies must have brown noses.

Size: About 41 cms (16 ins) at withers. This allows for slight variation below in the case of a bitch and above in the case of a dog.

Weight: 8–10 kgs (18–23 lbs).

Faults: Any departure from the foregoing points should be considered a fault and the seriousness with which the fault should be regarded should be in exact proportion to its degree.

Note: Male animals should have two apparently normal testicles fully descended into the scrotum.

underline. Body slightly greater in length than height.

Hindquarters: Muscular and moderate length, arched loin with curved topline immediately above loins. Hindlegs have appearance of being longer than forelegs. Hocks strong and well let down, turning neither in nor out.

Feet: Long harefeet with thick and well closed up pads.

Tail: Moderate length, thick at root, tapering to a point and gracefully curved. Set-on low, never carried over back.

Handlers should be thoroughly familiar with the breed standard so that they understand what judges are looking for and can present their dogs in the best possible way.

WHERE TO BEGIN?

If you are convinced that the Bedlington Terrier is the ideal dog for you, it's time to learn about where to find a puppy and what to look for. Locating a litter of Bedlington Terriers will require some homework on your part, as the breed is not too populous. You should enquire about breeders who enjoy a good reputation in the breed. New owners should have as many questions as they have doubts. An established breeder is indeed the one to answer your four million questions and make you comfortable with your choice of the Bedlington Terrier.

When choosing a breeder, reputation is much more important than convenience of location. Fortunately, the majority of Bedlington Terrier breeders is devoted to the breed and its well-being. New owners should have little problem finding a reputable breeder who doesn't live on the other side of the country (or in a different country). The Kennel Club is able to recommend breeders of quality Bedlington Terriers, as can any local all-breed club or Bedlington Terrier club.

Potential owners are encour-aged to attend dog shows to see the Bedlington Terriers in action, to meet the owners and handlers firsthand and to get an idea of what this 'darling little lamb' looks like outside a photographer's lens. Provided you approach the handlers when they are not terribly busy with the dogs, most are more than willing to answer questions, recommend breeders and give advice.

Once you have contacted and met a breeder or two and made your choice about which breeder is best suited to your needs, it's time to visit the litter. Keep in mind that many top breeders have waiting lists. Sometimes new

PUPPY SELECTION

Your selection of a good puppy can be determined by your needs. A show potential or a good pet? It is your choice. Every puppy, however, should be of good temperament. Although show-quality puppies are bred and raised with emphasis on physical conformation, responsible breeders strive for equally good temperament. Do not buy from a breeder who concentrates solely on physical beauty at the expense of personality.

owners have to wait as long as two years for a puppy. If you are really committed to the breeder whom you've selected, then you will wait (and hope for an early arrival!).

Since you are likely to be choosing a Bedlington Terrier as a pet dog and not a show dog, you simply should select a pup that is friendly, attractive and healthy. Bedlington Terriers generally have small litters, averaging three to four puppies, so selection is limited once you have located a desirable litter. Always check the bite of your selected puppy to be sure that it is neither overshot nor undershot. This may not be too noticeable on a young puppy, but will become more evident as the puppy gets older.

Breeders commonly allow visitors to see their litters by around the fifth or sixth week, and puppies leave for their new homes between the eighth and tenth week. Breeders who permit their puppies to leave early are more interested in your pounds than in their puppies' well-being. Puppies need to learn the rules of the pack from their dams, and most dams continue teaching the pups manners and dos and don'ts until around the eighth week. Breeders spend significant amounts of time with the Bedlington Terrier toddlers so that the pups are able to interact with the 'other species,' i.e. humans.

PREPARING FOR PUP

Unfortunately, when a puppy is bought by someone who does not take into consideration the time and attention that dog ownership requires, it is the puppy who suffers when he is either abandoned or placed in a shelter by a frustrated owner. So all of the 'homework' you do in preparation for your pup's arrival will benefit you both. The more informed you are, the more you will know what to expect and the better equipped you will be to handle the ups and downs of raising a puppy. Hopefully, everyone in the household is willing to do his part in raising and caring for the pup. The anticipation of owning a dog often brings a lot of promises from excited family members: 'I will walk him every day,' 'I will feed him,' 'I will house-train him,' etc., but these things take time and effort, and promises can easily be forgotten once the novelty of the new pet has worn off.

DID YOU KNOW?
You should not even think about buying a puppy that looks sick, undernourished, overly frightened or nervous. Sometimes a timid puppy will warm up to you after a 30-minute 'let's-get-acquainted' session.

decided which characteristics you want in a dog and what type of dog will best fit into your family and lifestyle. If you have selected a breeder, you have gone a step further—you have done your research and found a responsible, conscientious person who breeds quality Bedlington Terriers and who should become a reliable source of help as you and your puppy adjust to life together. If you have observed a litter in

While your puppy may not be a piano virtuoso, he will certainly be a first-class snooper! All puppies are curious, but this trait is especially prevalent in the Bedlington Terrier, who wants to learn everything about his surroundings.

Given the long history that dogs and humans have, bonding between the two species is natural but must be nurtured. A well-bred, well-socialised Bedlington Terrier pup wants nothing more than to be near you and please you.

COMMITMENT OF OWNERSHIP
After considering all of these factors, you have most likely already made some very important decisions about selecting your puppy. You have chosen a Bedlington Terrier, which means that you have

action, you have obtained a firsthand look at the dynamics of a puppy 'pack' and, thus, you have learned about each pup's individual personality—perhaps you have even found one that particularly appeals to you.

However, even if you have not yet found the Bedlington Terrier puppy of your dreams, observing pups will help you learn to recognise certain behaviour and to determine what a pup's behaviour indicates about his temperament. You will be able to pick out which pups are the leaders, which ones are less outgoing, which ones are confident, which ones are shy, playful, friendly, aggressive, etc. Male Bedlingtons tend to be more aggressive than females when it comes to meeting other dogs. This is a natural terrier trait that should be considered when selecting a pup. Equally as

PUPPY APPEARANCE

Your puppy should have a well-fed appearance but not a distended abdomen, which may indicate worms or incorrect feeding, or both. The body should be firm, with a solid feel. The skin of the abdomen should be pale pink and clean, without signs of scratching or rash. Check the hind legs to make certain that dewclaws were removed, if any were present at birth.

important, you will learn to recognise what a healthy pup should look and act like. All of these things will help you in your search, and when you find the Bedlington Terrier that was meant for you, you will know it!

Researching your breed, selecting a responsible breeder and observing as many pups as possible are all important steps on

You should take time in selecting your Bedlington Terrier puppy. Much can be learned about each pup's personality by watching the littermates interact with each other.

BOY OR GIRL?

An important consideration to be discussed is the sex of your puppy. For a family companion, a bitch may be the better choice, considering the female's inbred concern for all young creatures and her accompanying tolerance and patience. It is always advisable to spay a pet bitch, which may guarantee her a longer life.

that buying a puppy should be fun—it should not be so serious and so much work. Keep in mind that your puppy is not a cuddly stuffed toy or decorative lawn ornament; rather, he is a living creature that will become a real member of your family. You will come to realise that, while buying a puppy is a pleasurable and exciting endeavour, it is not something to be taken lightly. Relax…the fun will start when the pup comes home!

Always keep in mind that a puppy is nothing more than a baby in a furry disguise…a baby who is virtually helpless in a human world and who trusts his owner for fulfilment of his basic needs for survival. In addition to food, water and shelter, your pup needs care, protection, guidance

the way to dog ownership. It may seem like a lot of effort…and you have not even taken the pup home yet! Remember, though, you cannot be too careful when it comes to deciding on the type of dog you want and finding out about your prospective pup's background. Buying a puppy is not—or should not be—just another whimsical purchase. This is one instance in which you actually do get to choose your own family! You may be thinking

INSURANCE

Many good breeders will offer you insurance with your new puppy, which is an excellent idea. The first few weeks of insurance will probably be covered free of charge or with only minimal cost, allowing you to take up the policy when this expires. If you own a pet dog, it is sensible to take out such a policy as veterinary fees can be high, although routine vaccinations and boosters are not covered. Look carefully at the many options open to you before deciding which suits you best.

DOCUMENTATION

Two important documents you will get from the breeder are the pup's pedigree and registration certificate. The breeder should register the litter and each pup with The Kennel Club, and it is necessary for you to have the paperwork if you plan on showing or breeding in the future.

Make sure you know the breeder's intentions on which type of registration he will obtain for the pup. There are limited registrations which may prohibit the dog from being shown, bred or competing in non-conformation trials such as Working or Agility if the breeder feels that the pup is not of sufficient quality to do so. There is also a type of registration that will permit the dog in non-conformation competition only.

On the reverse side of the registration certificate, the new owner can find the transfer section, which must be signed by the breeder.

YOUR SCHEDULE . . .

If you lead an erratic, unpredictable life, with daily or weekly changes in your work requirements, consider the problems of owning a puppy. The new puppy has to be fed regularly, socialised (loved, petted, handled, introduced to other people) and, most importantly, allowed to visit outdoors for toilet training. As the dog gets older, it can be more tolerant of deviations in its feeding and toilet relief.

and love. If you are not prepared to commit to this, then you are not prepared to own a dog.

Wait a minute, you say. How hard could this be? All of my neighbours own dogs and they seem to be doing just fine. Why should I have to worry about all of this? Well, you should not worry about it; in fact, you will probably find that once your Bedlington Terrier pup gets used to his new home, he will fall into his place in the family quite naturally. However, it never hurts

The cast on this young Bedlington's leg is a testament to the trouble that puppies can get into. Provide supervision to ensure that accidents don't happen.

ARE YOU A FIT OWNER?
If the breeder from whom you are buying a puppy asks you a lot of personal questions, do not be insulted. Such a breeder wants to be sure that you will be a fit provider for his puppy.

to emphasise the commitment of dog ownership. With some time and patience, it is really not too difficult to raise a curious and exuberant Bedlington Terrier pup to be a well-adjusted and well-mannered adult dog—a dog that could be your most loyal friend.

PREPARING PUPPY'S PLACE IN YOUR HOME
Researching your breed and finding a breeder are only two aspects of the homework you will have to do before taking your Bedlington Terrier puppy home. You will also have to prepare your home and family for the new addition. Much as you would prepare a nursery for a newborn

baby, you will need to designate a place in your home that will be the puppy's own. How you prepare your home will depend on how much freedom the dog will be allowed. Whatever you decide, you must ensure that he has a place that he can 'call his own.'

When you bring your new puppy into your home, you are bringing him into what will become his home as well.

INHERIT THE MIND
In order to know whether or not a puppy will fit into your lifestyle, you need to assess his personality. A good way to do this is to interact with his parents. Your pup inherits not only his appearance but also his personality and temperament from the sire and dam. If the parents are fearful or overly aggressive, these same traits may likely show up in your puppy.

An open fireplace looks inviting but spells danger...the importance of puppy-proofing cannot be stressed enough!

Obviously, you did not buy a puppy with the intentions of catering to his every whim and allowing him to 'rule the roost,' but in order for a puppy to grow into a stable, well-adjusted dog, he has to feel comfortable in his surroundings. Remember, he is leaving the warmth and security of his mother and littermates, as well as the familiarity of the only place he has ever known, so it is important to make his transition as easy as possible. By preparing a place in your home for the puppy, you are making him feel as welcome as possible in a strange new place. It should not take him long to get used to it, but the sudden shock of being transplanted is somewhat traumatic for a young pup.

FEEDING TIPS
You will probably start feeding your pup the same food that he has been getting from the breeder; the breeder should give you a few days' supply to start you off. Although you should not give your pup too many treats, you will want to have puppy treats on hand for coaxing, training, rewards, etc. Be careful, though, as a small pup's calorie requirements are relatively low and a few treats can add up to almost a full day's worth of calories without the required nutrition.

PUPPY PERSONALITY
When a litter becomes available to you, choosing a pup out of all those adorable faces will not be an easy task! Sound temperament is of utmost importance, but each pup has its own personality and some may be better suited to you than others. A feisty, independent pup will do well in a home with older children and adults, while quiet, shy puppies will thrive in a home with minimal noise and distractions. Your breeder knows the pups best and should be able to guide you in the right direction.

Imagine how a small child would feel in the same situation—that is how your puppy must be feeling. It is up to you to reassure him and to let him know, 'Little chap, you are going to like it here!'

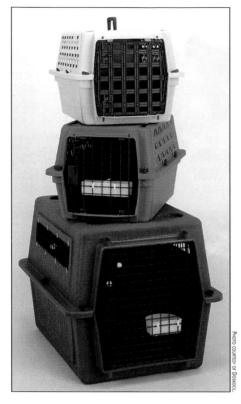

PHOTO COURTESY OF DOSKOCIL.

WHAT YOU SHOULD BUY

CRATE

To someone unfamiliar with the use of crates in dog training, it may seem like punishment to shut a dog in a crate, but this is not the case at all. Although all breeders do not advocate crate training, more and more breeders and trainers are recommending crates as preferred tools for show puppies as well as pet puppies. Crates are not cruel—crates have many humane and highly effective uses in dog care and training. For example, crate training is a very popular and very successful house-training method. In addition, a crate can keep your dog safe during travel and, perhaps most importantly, a crate provides your dog with a place of his own in your home. It serves as a 'doggie bedroom' of sorts—your Bedlington Terrier can curl up in his crate when he wants to sleep or when he just needs a break. Many dogs sleep in their crates overnight. With soft bedding and his favourite toy, a crate becomes a cosy pseudo-den for your dog. Like his ancestors, he too will seek out the comfort and retreat of a den—you just happen to be providing him with something a little more luxurious than what his early ancestors enjoyed.

As far as purchasing a crate, the type that you buy is up to you. It will most likely be one of the two most popular types: wire or fibreglass. There are advantages and disadvantages to each type. For example, a wire crate is more open, allowing the air to flow through and affording the dog a view of what is going on around him, while a fibreglass crate is sturdier. Both can double as travel crates, providing protection for the dog. The size of the crate is another thing to consider. Puppies do not stay puppies forever—in fact, sometimes it seems as if they grow right before your eyes. A very small crate may be fine for a very young Bedlington Terrier pup, but it will not do him much good for long! Unless you have the money and the inclination to buy a new crate every time your pup has a growth spurt, it is better to get one that will accommodate your dog both as a pup and at full size. A medium-size crate will be necessary for a fully-grown Bedlington Terrier, who stands approximately 41 cms (16 ins) high.

BEDDING

Veterinary bedding in the dog's crate will help the dog feel more at home, and you may also like to pop in a small blanket. First, this will take the place of the leaves, twigs, etc., that the pup would use in the wild to make a den; the pup can make his own 'burrow' in the crate. Although your pup is far removed from his den-making ancestors, the denning instinct is still a part of his genetic makeup. Second, until you take your pup home, he has been sleeping amidst the warmth of his mother and littermates, and while a blanket is not the same as a warm, breathing body, it still provides heat and something with which to snuggle. You will want to wash your pup's bedding frequently in case he has a toileting 'accident' in his crate, and replace or remove any blanket that becomes ragged and starts to fall apart.

CRATE TRAINING TIPS

During crate training, you should partition off the section of the crate in which the pup stays. If he is given too big an area, this will hinder your training efforts. Crate training is based on the fact that a dog does not like to soil his sleeping quarters, so it is ineffective to keep a pup in a crate that is so big that he can eliminate in one end and get far enough away from it to sleep. Also, you want to make the crate den-like for the pup. Blankets and a favourite toy will make the crate cosy for the small pup; as he grows, you may want to evict some of his 'roommates' to make more room.

It will take some coaxing at first, but be patient. Given some time to get used to it, your pup will adapt to his new home-within-a-home quite nicely.

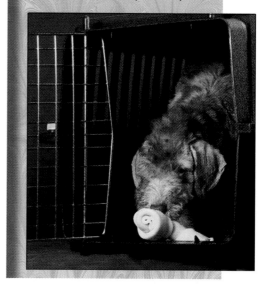

TOYS, TOYS, TOYS!

With a big variety of dog toys available, and so many that look like they would be a lot of fun for a dog, be careful in your selection. It is amazing what a set of puppy teeth can do to an innocent-looking toy, so, obviously, safety is a major consideration. Be sure to choose the most durable products that you can find. Hard nylon bones and toys are a safe bet, and many of them are offered in different scents and flavours that will be sure to capture your dog's attention. It is always fun to play a game of catch with your dog, and there are balls and flying discs that are specially made to withstand dog teeth.

Toys

Toys are a must for dogs of all ages, especially for curious playful pups. Puppies are the 'children' of the dog world, and what child does not love toys? Chew toys provide enjoyment for both dog and owner—your dog will enjoy playing with his favourite toys, while you will enjoy the fact that they distract him from chewing on your expensive shoes and leather sofa. Puppies love to chew; in fact, chewing is a physical need for pups as they are teething, and everything looks appetising! The full range of your possessions— from old tea towel to Oriental carpet—are fair game in the eyes of a teething pup. Puppies are not all that discerning when it comes to finding something literally to 'sink their teeth into'—everything tastes great!

Like most other terriers, Bedlington Terrier puppies are fairly aggressive chewers and only the hardest, strongest toys should be offered to them. Breeders advise owners to resist stuffed toys, because they can become de-stuffed in no time. The overly excited pup may ingest the stuffing, which is neither digestible nor nutritious.

Similarly, squeaky toys are quite popular, but must be avoided for the Bedlington Terrier. Perhaps a squeaky toy can be used as an aid in training, but not for free play. If a pup 'disembowels' one of these, the small plastic squeaker inside can be dangerous if swallowed. Monitor the condition of all your pup's toys carefully and get rid of any that have been chewed to the point of becoming potentially dangerous.

Be careful of natural bones, which have a tendency to splinter into sharp, dangerous pieces. Also be careful of rawhide, which can turn into pieces that are easy to swallow and become a mushy mess on your carpet.

PLAY'S THE THING

Teaching the puppy to play with his toys in running and fetching games is an ideal way to help the puppy develop muscle, learn motor skills and bond with you, his owner and master.

He also needs to learn how to inhibit his bite reflex and never to use his teeth on people, forbidden objects and other animals in play. Whenever you play with your puppy, you make the rules. This becomes an important message to your puppy in teaching him that you are the pack leader and control everything he does in life. Once your dog accepts you as his leader, your relationship with him will be cemented for life.

MENTAL AND DENTAL

Toys not only help your puppy get the physical and mental stimulation he needs but also provide a great way to keep his teeth clean. Hard rubber or nylon toys, especially those constructed with grooves, are designed to scrape away plaque, preventing bad breath and gum infection.

LEAD

A nylon lead is probably the best option, as it is the most resistant to puppy teeth should your pup take a liking to chewing on his lead. Of course, this is a habit that

Pet shops usually stock large assortments of leads. You are sure to find one that suits your Bedlington Terrier.

COLLAR

Your pup should get used to wearing a collar all the time since you will want to attach his ID tags to it; plus, you have to attach the lead to something! A lightweight nylon collar is a good choice. Make certain that the collar fits snugly enough so that the pup cannot wriggle out of it, but is loose enough so that it will not be

should be nipped in the bud, but, if your pup likes to chew on his lead, he has a very slim chance of being able to chew through the strong nylon. Nylon leads are also lightweight, which is good for a young Bedlington Terrier who is just getting used to the idea of walking on a lead. For everyday walking and safety purposes, the nylon lead is a good choice. As your pup grows up and gets used to walking on the lead, you may want to purchase a flexible lead. These leads allow you to extend the length to give the dog a broader area to explore or to shorten the length to keep the dog near you. Of course, there are leads designed for training purposes and specially made leather harnesses, but these are not necessary for routine walks.

FINANCIAL RESPONSIBILITY

Grooming tools, collars, leashes, dog beds and, of course, toys will be an expense to you when you first obtain your pup, and the cost will continue throughout your dog's lifetime. If your puppy damages or destroys your possessions (as most puppies surely will!) or something belonging to a neighbour, you can calculate additional expense. There is also flea and pest control, which every dog owner faces more than once. You must be able to handle the financial responsibility of owning a dog.

CHOOSE AN APPROPRIATE COLLAR

The **BUCKLE COLLAR** is the standard collar used for everyday purposes. Be sure that you adjust the buckle on growing puppies. Check it every day. It can become too tight overnight! These collars can be made of leather or nylon. Attach your dog's identification tags to this collar.

The **CHOKE COLLAR**, although not recommended for use with a Bedlington, is the usual collar recommended for training. It is constructed of highly polished steel so that it slides easily through the stainless steel loop. The idea is that the dog controls the pressure around its neck and he will stop pulling if the collar becomes uncomfortable. A choke collar should never be left on a dog when not training.

The **HALTER** is for a trained dog that has to be restrained to prevent running away, chasing a cat and the like. Considered the most humane of all collars, it is frequently used on smaller dogs for which collars are not comfortable.

Purchase sturdy containers for water and food. The more durable the bowls, the longer they will last.

PHOTO COURTESY OF MIKKI PET PRODUCTS.

uncomfortably tight around the pup's neck. You should be able to fit a finger between the pup's neck and the collar. It may take some time for your pup to get used to wearing the collar, but soon he will not even notice that it is there. Choke collars are made for training, but should only be used by experienced handlers and are not recommended for use on small dogs and coated breeds like the Bedlington.

FOOD AND WATER BOWLS

Your pup will need two bowls, one for food and one for water. You may want two sets of bowls, one for indoors and one for outdoors, depending on where the dog will be fed and where he will be spending time. Stainless steel or sturdy plastic bowls are popular choices. Plastic bowls are more chewable, but dogs tend not to chew on the steel variety, which can be sterilised. It is important to buy sturdy bowls since anything is in danger of being chewed by puppy teeth and you do not want your dog to be constantly chewing apart his bowl (for his safety and for your purse!).

CLEANING SUPPLIES

Until a pup is house-trained you will be doing a lot of cleaning. 'Accidents' will occur, which is acceptable in the beginning stages of toilet training because the puppy does not know any better.

All you can do is be prepared to clean up any accidents as soon as they happen. Old rags, towels, newspapers and a safe disinfectant are good to have on hand.

BEYOND THE BASICS

The items previously discussed are the bare necessities. You will find out what else you need as you go along—grooming supplies, flea/tick protection, baby gates to partition a room, etc. These things will vary depending on your

It is your responsibility to clean up after your Bedlington has relieved itself. Pet shops have various aids to assist in the clean-up task.

QUALITY FOOD

The cost of food must be mentioned. All dogs need a good-quality food with an adequate supply of protein to develop their bones and muscles properly. Most dogs are not picky eaters but, unless fed properly, can quickly succumb to skin problems.

situation, but it is important that you have everything you need to feed and make your Bedlington Terrier comfortable in his first few days at home.

PUPPY-PROOFING YOUR HOME

Aside from making sure that your Bedlington Terrier will be comfortable in your home, you also have to make sure that your home is safe for your Bedlington Terrier. This means taking precautions that your pup will not get into anything he should not get into and that there is nothing within his reach that may harm him should he sniff it, chew it, inspect it, etc. This probably

An electrical cord can pose a danger should the puppy decide to taste it—and who is going to convince a pup that it would not make a great chew toy? Cords should be fastened tightly against the wall. If your dog is going to spend time in a crate, make sure that there is nothing near his crate that he can reach if he sticks his curious little nose or paws through the openings. Just as you would with a child, keep all household cleaners and chemicals where the pup cannot reach them.

It is also important to make sure that the outside of your home is safe. Of course, your puppy should never be unsupervised, but a pup let loose in the garden will want to run and explore, and he should be granted that freedom. Do not let a fence give you a false sense of security; you would be surprised at how crafty (and persistent) a dog can be in working out how to dig under and squeeze his way through small holes, or to jump or climb over a

NATURAL TOXINS
Examine your grass and garden landscaping before bringing your puppy home. Many varieties of plants have leaves, stems or flowers that are toxic if ingested, and you can depend on a curious puppy to investigate them. Ask your vet for information on poisonous plants or research them at your library.

seems obvious since, while you are primarily concerned with your pup's safety, at the same time you do not want your belongings to be ruined. Breakables should be placed out of reach if your dog is to have full run of the house. If he is to be limited to certain places within the house, keep any potentially dangerous items in the 'off-limits' areas.

CHEMICAL TOXINS
Scour your garage for potential puppy dangers. Remove weed killers, pesticides and antifreeze materials. Antifreeze is highly toxic and even a few drops can kill an adult dog. The sweet taste attracts the animal, who will quickly consume it from the floor or curbside.

fence. The Bedlington is a talented digger and will engage in his art whenever he is so inspired...or completely uninspired and bored!

The remedy is to make the fence well embedded into the ground and high enough so that it really is impossible for your dog to get over it (about 3 metres should suffice). Be sure to repair or secure any gaps in the fence. Check the fence periodically to ensure that it is in good shape and make repairs as needed; a very determined pup may return to the same spot to 'work on it' until he is able to get through.

FIRST TRIP TO THE VET

You have selected your puppy, and your home and family are ready. Now all you have to do is collect your Bedlington Terrier from the breeder and the fun begins, right? Well...not so fast. Something else you need to plan is your pup's first trip to the veterinary surgeon. Perhaps the breeder can recommend someone in the area who specialises in terriers, or maybe you know some other Bedlington Terrier owners who can suggest a good vet. Either way, you should have an appointment arranged for your pup before you pick him up.

The pup's first visit will consist of an overall examination to make sure that the pup does not have any problems that are

not apparent to the owner. The veterinary surgeon will also set up a schedule for the pup's vaccinations; the breeder will inform you of which ones the pup has already received and the vet can continue from there.

TOXIC PLANTS

Many plants can be toxic to dogs. If you see your dog carrying a piece of vegetation in his mouth, approach him in a quiet, disinterested manner, avoid eye contact, pet him and gradually remove the plant from his mouth. Alternatively, offer him a treat and maybe he'll drop the plant on his own accord. Be sure no toxic plants are growing in your own garden.

INTRODUCTION TO THE FAMILY

Everyone in the house will be excited about the puppy's coming home and will want to pet him and play with him, but it is best to make the introduction low-key so as not to overwhelm the puppy. He is apprehensive already. It is the first time he has been separated from his mother and the breeder, and the ride to your home is likely to be the first time he has been in a car. The last thing you want to do is smother him, as this will only frighten him further. This is not to say that human contact is not extremely necessary at this stage, because this is the time when a connection between the pup and his human family is formed. Gentle petting and soothing words should help console him, as well as just putting him down and letting him explore on his own (under your watchful eye, of course).

The pup may approach the family members or may busy himself with exploring for a

Give your Bedlington pup time to adjust to his new home. Do not overwhelm him, but give him encouragement and praise as he settles in.

PUPPY-PROOFING

Thoroughly puppy-proof your house before bringing your puppy home. Never use cockroach or rodent poisons in any area accessible to the puppy. Avoid the use of toilet cleaners. Most dogs are born with 'toilet sonar' and will take a drink if the lid is left open. Also keep the rubbish secured and out of reach.

while. Gradually, each person should spend some time with the pup, one at a time, crouching down to get as close to the pup's level as possible, letting him sniff their hands and petting him gently. He definitely needs human attention and he needs to be touched—this is how to form an immediate bond. Just remember that the pup is experiencing many things for the first time, at the same time. There are new people, new noises, new smells and new things to investigate, so be gentle, be affectionate and be as comforting as you can be.

PUP'S FIRST NIGHT HOME

You have travelled home with your new charge safely in his crate. He's been to the vet for a thorough check-up; he's been weighed, his papers have been examined and perhaps he's even been vaccinated and wormed as well. He's met (and licked!) the whole family, including the excited children and the less-than-happy cat. He's explored his area, his new bed, the garden and anywhere else he's been permitted. He's eaten his first meal at home and relieved himself in the proper place. He's heard lots of new sounds, smelled new friends and seen more of the outside world than ever before... and that was just the first day! He's worn out and is ready for bed...or so you think!

It's puppy's first night home and you are ready to say 'Good night.' Keep in mind that this is his first night ever to be sleeping alone. His dam and littermates are no longer at paw's length and he's a bit scared, cold and lonely. Be reassuring to your new family member, but this is not the time to spoil him and give in to his inevitable whining.

Puppies whine. They whine to let others know where they are and hopefully to get company out of it. Place your pup in his new bed or crate in his designated area and close the door. Mercifully, he may fall asleep without a peep. When the inevitable occurs, however, ignore the whining—he is fine. Be strong and keep his interest in mind. Do not allow yourself to feel guilty and visit the pup. He will fall asleep eventually.

Many breeders recommend placing a piece of bedding from the pup's former home in his new bed so that he recognises and is comforted by the scent of his littermates. Others still advise placing a hot water bottle in the bed for warmth. The latter may be a good idea provided the pup doesn't attempt to suckle—he'll get good and wet, and may not fall asleep so fast.

Puppy's first night can be somewhat stressful for both the pup and his new family.

A Bedlington Terrier that is properly socialised as a pup will grow up into a friendly dog that is eager to make new acquaintances.

Remember that you are setting the tone of night-time at your house. Unless you want to play with your pup every night at 10 p.m., midnight and 2 a.m., don't initiate the habit. Your family will thank you, and so will your pup!

PROPER SOCIALISATION

The socialisation period for puppies is from age 8 to 16 weeks. This is the time when puppies need to leave their birth family and take up residence with their new owners, where they will meet many new people, other pets, etc. Failure to be adequately socialised can cause the dog to grow up fearing others and being shy and unfriendly due to a lack of self-confidence.

PREVENTING PUPPY PROBLEMS

SOCIALISATION
Now that you have done all of the preparatory work and have helped your pup get accustomed to his

MEET THE WORLD

Thorough socialisation includes not only meeting new people but also being introduced to new experiences such as riding in the car, having his coat brushed, hearing the television, walking in a crowd—the list is endless. The more your pup experiences, and the more positive the experiences are, the less of a shock and the less frightening it will be for your pup to encounter new things.

new home and family, it is about time for you to have some fun! Socialising your Bedlington Terrier pup gives you the opportunity to show off your new friend, and your pup gets to reap the benefits of being an adorable furry creature that people will want to pet and, in general, think is absolutely precious!

Besides getting to know his new family, your puppy should be exposed to other people, animals and situations. This will help him become well adjusted as he grows up and less prone to being timid or fearful of the new things he will encounter. Of course, he must not come into close contact with dogs you don't know well until his course of injections is fully complete.

Your pup's socialisation began with the breeder, but now it is your responsibility to continue it. The socialisation he receives until the age of 12 weeks is the most critical, as this is the time when he forms his impressions of the outside world. Be especially careful during the eight-to-ten-week period, also known as the fear period. The interaction he receives during this time should be gentle and reassuring. Lack of socialisation, and/or negative experiences during the socialisation period, can manifest itself in fear and aggression as the dog grows up. Your puppy needs lots of positive interaction, which of

MANNERS MATTER

During the socialisation process, a puppy should meet people, experience different environments and definitely be exposed to other canines. Through playing and interacting with other dogs, your puppy will learn lessons, ranging from controlling the pressure of his jaws by biting his littermates to the inner-workings of the canine pack that he will apply to his human relationships for the rest of his life. That is why removing a puppy from its litter too early (before eight weeks) can be detrimental to the pup's development.

course includes human contact, affection, handling and exposure to other animals.

Once your pup has received his necessary vaccinations, feel free to take him out and about (on his lead, of course). Walk him around the neighbourhood, take him on your daily errands, let people pet him, let him meet other dogs and pets, etc. Puppies

Decide on the house rules and enforce them early on. If you do not want your Bedlington to share your favourite chair as an adult, don't allow him to do so as a puppy.

do not have to try to make friends; there will be no shortage of people who will want to introduce themselves. Just make sure that you carefully supervise each meeting. If the neighbourhood children want to say hello, for example, that is great— children and pups most often make fine companions. However, sometimes an excited child can unintentionally handle a pup too roughly, or an overzealous pup can playfully nip a little too hard. You want to make socialisation experiences positive ones. What a pup learns during this very formative stage will affect his attitude toward future encounters. You want your dog to be comfortable around everyone. A pup that has a bad experience with a child may grow up to be a dog that is shy around or aggressive toward children.

CONSISTENCY IN TRAINING

Dogs, being pack animals, naturally need a leader, or else they try to establish dominance in their packs. When you welcome a dog into your family, the choice of who becomes the leader and who becomes the 'pack' is entirely up to you! Your pup's intuitive quest for dominance, coupled with the fact that it is nearly impossible to look at an adorable Bedlington Terrier pup with his 'baby lamb' face and not cave in, give the pup almost an unfair advantage in getting the upper hand! A pup will definitely test the waters to see what he can and cannot do. Do not give in to those pleading eyes—stand your ground when it comes to disciplining the pup and make sure that all family members do the same. It will only confuse the pup if Mother tells him to get off the sofa when he is used to sitting up there with Father to watch the nightly news. Avoid discrepancies by having all members of the household decide on the rules before the pup even comes home…and be consistent in enforcing them! Early training shapes the dog's personality, so you cannot be unclear in what you expect.

COMMON PUPPY PROBLEMS

The best way to prevent puppy problems is to be proactive in stopping an undesirable behaviour as soon as it starts. The old saying 'You can't teach an old dog new tricks' does not necessarily hold true, but it is true that it is much easier to discourage bad behaviour in a young developing pup than to wait until the pup's bad behaviour becomes the adult dog's bad habit. There are some problems that are especially prevalent in puppies as they develop.

NIPPING

As puppies start to teethe, they feel the need to sink their teeth into anything available...unfortunately, that usually includes your fingers, arms, hair and toes. You may find this behaviour cute for the first five seconds...until you feel just how sharp those puppy teeth are. Nipping is something you want to discourage immediately and consistently with a firm 'No!' (or whatever number of firm 'Nos' it takes for him to understand that you mean business). Then, replace your finger with an appropriate chew toy. While this behaviour is merely annoying when the dog is young, it can become dangerous as your Bedlington Terrier's adult teeth grow in and his jaws develop, and he continues to think it is okay to gnaw on human appendages. Your Bedlington Terrier does not mean any harm with a friendly nip, but he also does not know the strength of his terrier jaws.

CRYING/WHINING

Your pup will often cry, whine, whimper, howl or make some type of commotion when he is left alone. This is basically his way of calling out for attention to make sure that you know he is there

TRAINING TIP

Training your puppy takes much patience and can be frustrating at times, but you should see results from your efforts. If you have a puppy that seems untrainable, take him to a trainer or behaviourist. The dog may have a personality problem that requires the help of a professional, or perhaps you need help in learning how to train your dog.

and that you have not forgotten about him. Your puppy feels insecure when he is left alone, when you are out of the house and he is in his crate or when you are in another part of the house and he cannot see you. The noise he is making is an expression of the anxiety he feels at being alone,

so he needs to be taught that being alone is okay. You are not actually training the dog to stop making noise; rather, you are training him to feel comfortable when he is alone and thus removing the need for him to make the noise. This is where the crate with cosy bedding and a toy comes in handy. You want to know that your pup is safe when you are not there to supervise, and you know that he will be safe in his crate rather than roaming freely about the house. In order for the pup to stay in his crate without making a fuss, he first needs to be comfortable in his crate. On that note, it is extremely important that the crate is never used as a form of punishment; this will cause the pup to view the crate as a negative place, rather than as a place of his own for safety and retreat.

Accustom the pup to the crate in short, gradually increasing time intervals in which you put him in the crate, maybe with a treat, and stay in the room with him. If he cries or makes a fuss, do not go to him, but stay in his sight. Gradually he will realise that staying in his crate is all right without your help, and it will not be so traumatic for him when you are not around. You may want to leave the radio on softly when you leave the house; the sound of human voices may be comforting to him.

CHEWING TIPS

Chewing goes hand in hand with nipping in the sense that a teething puppy is always looking for a way to soothe his aching gums. In this case, instead of chewing on you, he may have taken a liking to your favourite shoe or something else which he should not be chewing. Again, realise that this is a normal canine behaviour that does not need to be discouraged, only redirected. Your pup just needs to be taught what is acceptable to chew on and what is off limits. Consistently tell him NO when you catch him chewing on something forbidden and give him a chew toy. Conversely, praise him when you catch him chewing on something appropriate. In this way you are discouraging the inappropriate behaviour and reinforcing the desired behaviour. The puppy chewing should stop after his adult teeth have come in, but an adult dog continues to chew for various reasons—perhaps because he is bored, perhaps to relieve tension or perhaps he just likes to chew. That is why it is important to redirect his chewing when he is still young.

DIETARY AND FEEDING CONSIDERATIONS

Today the choices of food for your Bedlington Terrier are many and varied. There are simply dozens of brands of food in all sorts of flavours and textures, ranging from puppy diets to those for seniors. There are even hypoallergenic and low-calorie diets available. Because your Bedlington Terrier's food has a bearing on coat, health and temperament, it is essential that the most suitable diet is selected for a Bedlington Terrier of his age. It is fair to say, however, that even experienced owners can be perplexed by the enormous range of foods available. Only understanding what is best for your dog will help you reach an informed decision.

Dog foods are produced in three basic types: dried, semi-moist and tinned. Dried foods are useful for the cost-conscious, for overall they tend to be less expensive than semi-moist or tinned foods. Dried foods also contain the least fat and the most

preservatives. In general, tinned foods are made up of 60–70 percent water, while semi-moist ones often contain so much sugar that they are perhaps the least preferred by owners, even though their dogs seem to like them.

FEEDING TIP
You must store your dried dog food carefully. Open packages of dog food quickly lose their vitamin value, usually within 90 days of being opened. Mould spores and vermin could also contaminate the food.

FEEDING TIPS

Dog food must be at room temperature, neither too hot nor too cold. Fresh water, changed often and served in a clean bowl, is mandatory, especially when feeding dried food.

Never feed your dog from the table while you are eating, and never feed your dog leftovers from your own meal. They usually contain too much fat and too much seasoning.

Dogs must chew their food. Hard pellets are excellent; soups and slurries are to be avoided.

Don't add leftovers or any extras to normal dog food. The normal food is usually balanced, and adding something extra destroys the balance.

Except for age-related changes, dogs do not require dietary variations. They can be fed the same diet, day after day, without becoming ill.

When selecting your dog's diet, three stages of development must be considered: the puppy stage, the adult stage and the senior or veteran stage.

PUPPY STAGE

Puppies instinctively want to suck milk from their mother's teats; a normal puppy will exhibit this behaviour just a few moments following birth. If puppies do not attempt to suckle within the first half-hour or so, they should be encouraged to do so by placing them on the nipples, having selected ones with plenty of milk. This early milk supply is important in providing the essential colostrum, which protects the puppies during the first eight to ten weeks of their lives. Although a mother's milk is much better than any milk formula, despite there being some excellent ones available, if the puppies do not feed, the breeder will have to feed them by hand. For those with less experience,

TEST FOR PROPER DIET

A good test for proper diet is the colour, odour and firmness of your dog's stool. A healthy dog usually produces three semi-hard stools per day. The stools should have no unpleasant odour. They should be the same colour from excretion to excretion.

GRAIN-BASED DIETS

Some less expensive dog foods are based on grains and other plant proteins. While these products may appear to be attractively priced, many breeders prefer a diet based on animal proteins and believe that they are more conducive to your dog's health. Many grain-based diets rely on soy protein, which may cause flatulence (passing gas).

There are many cases, however, when your dog might require a special diet. These special requirements should only be recommended by your veterinary surgeon.

FOOD PREFERENCE

Selecting the best dried dog food is difficult. There is no majority consensus among veterinary scientists as to the value of nutrient analyses (protein, fat, fibre, moisture, ash, cholesterol, minerals, etc.). All agree that feeding trials are what matter, but you also have to consider the individual dog. The dog's weight, age and activity level, and what pleases his taste, all must be considered. It is probably best to take the advice of your veterinary surgeon. Every dog's dietary requirements vary, even during the lifetime of a particular dog.

If your dog is fed a good dried food, it does not require supplements of meat or vegetables. Dogs do appreciate a little variety in their diets, so you may choose to stay with the same brand but vary the flavour. Alternatively, you may wish to add a little flavoured stock to give a difference to the taste.

advice from a veterinary surgeon is important so that not only the right quantity of milk is fed but also that of correct quality, fed at suitably frequent intervals, usually every two hours during the first few days of life.

Puppies should be allowed to nurse from their mothers for about the first six weeks, although, starting around the third or fourth week, the breeder will begin to introduce small portions of suitable solid food. Most breeders like to introduce alternate milk and meat meals initially, building up to weaning time.

By the time the puppies are seven or a maximum of eight weeks old, they should be fully weaned and fed solely on a proprietary puppy food. Selection of the most suitable, good-quality diet at this time is essential, for a puppy's fastest growth rate is

THE CANINE GOURMET

Your dog does not prefer a fresh bone. Indeed, he wants it properly aged and, if given such a treat indoors, he is more likely to try to bury it in the carpet than he is to settle in for a good chew! If you have a garden, give him such delicacies outside and guide him to a place suitable for his 'bone yard.' He will carefully place the treasure in its earthy vault and seemingly forget about it. Trust me, his seeming distaste or lack of thanks for your thoughtfulness is not that at all. He will return in a few days to inspect the bone, perhaps to re-bury it, and when it is just right, he will relish it as much as you do that cooked-to-perfection steak. If he is in a concrete or bricked kennel run, he will be especially frustrated at the hopelessness of the situation. He will vacillate between ignoring it completely, giving it a few licks to speed the curing process with saliva, and trying to hide it behind the water bowl! When the bone has aged a bit, he will set to work on it.

TIPPING THE SCALES

Good nutrition is vital to your dog's health, but many people end up over-feeding or giving unnecessary supplements. Here are some common doggie diet don'ts:
- Adding milk, yoghurt and cheese to your dog's diet may seem like a good idea for coat and skin care, but dairy products are very fattening and can cause indigestion.
- Diets high in fat will not cause heart attacks in dogs but will certainly cause your dog to gain weight.
- Most importantly, don't assume your dog will simply stop eating once he doesn't need any more food. Given the chance, he will eat you out of house and home!

during the first year of life. Veterinary surgeons are usually able to offer advice in this regard and, although the frequency of meals will be reduced over time, only when a young dog has reached the age of about 12 months should an adult diet be

What are you feeding your dog?

Read the label on your dog food. Many dog foods only advise what 50—55% of the contents are, leaving the other 45% in doubt.

Calcium 1.3%
Fatty Acids 1.6%
Crude Fibre 4.6%
Moisture 11%
Crude Fat 14%
Crude Protein 22%

45.5% ? ? ?

DO DOGS HAVE TASTE BUDS?

Watching a dog 'wolf' or gobble his food, seemingly without chewing, leads an owner to wonder whether their dogs can taste anything. Yes, dogs have taste buds, with sensory perception of sweet, salty and sour. Puppies are born with fully mature taste buds.

veterinary surgeon or dietary specialist to recommend an acceptable maintenance diet. Major dog food manufacturers specialise in this type of food, and it is merely necessary for you to select the one best suited to your dog's needs. Active dogs may have different requirements than sedate dogs.

SENIOR DIETS

As dogs get older, their metabolism changes. The older dog usually exercises less, moves

fed. Puppy and junior diets should be well balanced for the needs of your dog so that, except in certain circumstances, additional vitamins, minerals and proteins will not be required.

ADULT DIETS

A dog is considered an adult when it has stopped growing, so in general the diet of a Bedlington Terrier can be changed to an adult one at around 12 months of age. Again you should rely upon your

'DOES THIS COLLAR MAKE ME LOOK FAT?'

While humans may obsess about how they look and how trim their bodies are, many people believe that extra weight on their dogs is a good thing. The truth is, pets should not be over- or under-weight, as both can lead to or signal sickness. In order to tell how fit your pet is, run your hands over his ribs. Are his ribs buried under a layer of fat or are they sticking out considerably? If your pet is within his normal weight range, you should be able to feel the ribs easily, but they should not protrude abnormally. If you stand above him, the outline of his body should resemble an hourglass. Some breeds do tend to be leaner while some are a bit stockier, but making sure your dog is the right weight for his breed will certainly contribute to his good health.

more slowly and sleeps more. This change in lifestyle and physiological performance requires a change in diet. Since these changes take place slowly, they might not be recognisable. What is easily recognisable is weight gain. By continuing to feed your dog an adult-maintenance diet when it is slowing down metabolically, your dog will gain weight. Obesity in an older dog compounds the health problems that already accompany old age.

As your dog gets older, few of his organs function up to par. The kidneys slow down and the intestines become less efficient. These age-related factors are best handled with a change in diet and a change in feeding schedule to give smaller portions that are more easily digested. There is no single best diet for every older dog. While many dogs do well on light or senior diets, other dogs do better on puppy diets or other special premium diets such as lamb and rice. Be sensitive to · your senior Bedlington Terrier's diet, as this will help control other problems that may arise with your old friend.

WATER

Just as your dog needs proper nutrition from his food, water is an essential 'nutrient' as well. Water keeps the dog's body properly hydrated and promotes normal function of the body's systems. During house-training it is necessary to keep an eye on how much water your Bedlington Terrier is drinking, but once he is

DRINK, DRANK, DRUNK— MAKE IT A DOUBLE

In both humans and dogs, as well as most living organisms, water forms the major part of nearly every body tissue. Naturally, we take water for granted, but without it, life as we know it would cease.

For dogs, water is needed to keep their bodies functioning biochemically. Additionally, water is needed to replace the water lost while panting. Unlike humans, who are able to sweat to dissipate heat, dogs must pant to cool down, thereby losing the vital water from their bodies needed to regulate their body temperatures. Humans lose electrolyte-containing products and other body-fluid components through sweating; dogs do not lose anything except water.

Water is essential always, but especially so when the weather is hot or humid or when your dog is exercising or working vigorously.

reliably trained he should have access to clean fresh water at all times, especially if you feed dried food. Make certain that the dog's water bowl is clean, and change the water often.

EXERCISE

The terrier breeds are active dogs that require considerable exercise to stay fit and mentally balanced. Regardless of breed, a sedentary lifestyle is as harmful to a dog as it is to a person, and, with the Bedlington Terrier, more is more when it comes to activity. Nonetheless, you don't have to be an Olympic athlete to provide your dog with a sufficient amount of exercise. Fortunately, those Bedlington limbs are short and you don't have to run ten kilometres a day to keep your chum fit. Exercising your Bedlington Terrier can be enjoyable and healthy for both of you. Brisk walks, once the puppy reaches three or four months of age, will stimulate heart rates and build muscle for both dog and owner. As the dog reaches adulthood, the speed and distance of the walks can be increased as long as they are both kept reasonable and comfortable for both of you.

Play sessions in the garden and letting the dog run free in the garden under your supervision also are sufficient forms of exercise for the Bedlington Terrier. Fetching games can be played indoors or out; these are excellent for giving your dog active play that he will enjoy. Chasing things that move comes naturally to dogs of all breeds, and the Bedlington is the king of the chase. If you choose to play games outdoors, you must have a securely fenced-in garden and/or have the dog attached to at least a 25-foot light line for security. You want your Bedlington Terrier to run, but not run away!

Bear in mind that an overweight dog should never be suddenly over-exercised; instead he should be encouraged to increase exercise slowly. Not only is exercise essential to keep the dog's body fit, it is essential to his mental well-being. A bored dog will find something to do, which often manifests itself in some type of destructive behaviour. In this sense, exercise is essential for the owner's mental well-being as well!

GROOMING

Most dogs, no matter how short the coat, will require some grooming so that you can have a dog that can live in the house with you, that will be a reputable family member, that is clean and that smells nice. Do be aware when considering a Bedlington Terrier as a pet that this is a breed that needs grooming. If the dog is not groomed, you will eventually have a matted dog who will no longer resemble the lamb-like look that appealed to you when you purchased your Bedlington. The plus side of a Bedlington is that, unlike most other breeds, he is a non-shedding dog. However, he does need grooming to eliminate the dead hair, as this is what will mat if not removed.

If you are purchasing your Bedlington as a show dog, he will need extensive grooming. This is a skill that is best learned from an experienced individual such as the breeder of your pup. This is also a skill which cannot be learned in an hour or even a day, as it takes time and experience to perfect the well-groomed dog for the show ring.

GROOMING EQUIPMENT

How much grooming equipment you purchase will depend on how much grooming you are going to do. Here are some basics:

- Natural bristle brush
- Slicker brush
- Metal comb
- Scissors
- Blaster
- Rubber mat
- Dog shampoo
- Spray hose attachment
- Ear cleaner
- Cotton wipes
- Towels
- Nail clippers
- Electric clippers
  with #5 & #15 blades

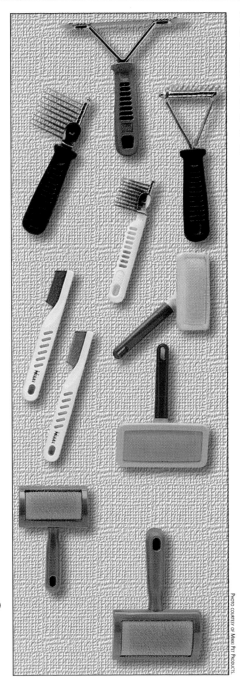

Your local pet shop should carry a variety of grooming tools. The tools you need for your Bedlington will vary, depending on if yours is a pet or show dog.

PHOTO COURTESY OF MIKKI PET PRODUCTS.

The ear before trimming.

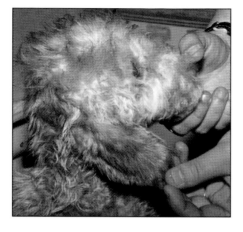

Cutting around the edge of the ear.

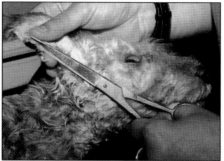

The finished ear.

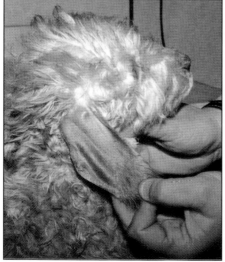

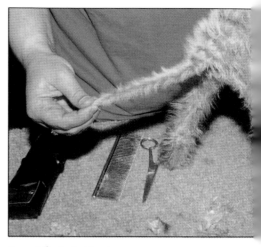

Puppy tail prior to trimming.

Putting the finishing touches to the tail.

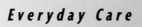

A puppy with the left leg untrimmed and the right leg trimmed.

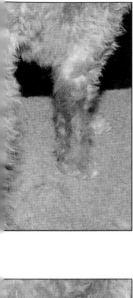

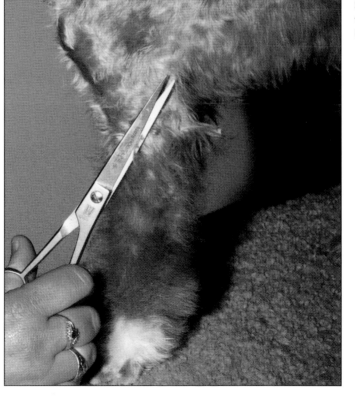

Scissors are used to neaten up the legs.

The facial hair is combed gently, using a comb with widely spaced teeth.

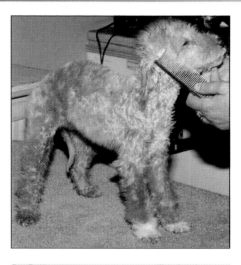

Trimming the puppy coat with electric clippers.

Use a specially formulated cleaner and cotton wipe around the eyes to clean the area and remove any tear stains.

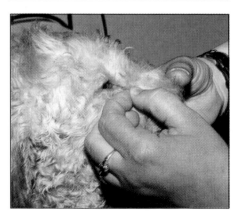

Since the vast majority of dog owners buys his dog for a companion rather than show dog, we will assume that you will be doing a pet clip for your dog. This is perfectly acceptable and relatively easy to do, and you will have a dog that looks like the proper Bedlington.

There is some basic equipment that you will need before starting. You will need a grooming table, which is a sturdy table with a non-skid surface covering the top. On this you will have an arm, or 'hanger,' with which you will attach the leash so that your dog can not jump off the table or lay down 'on the job,' as this makes grooming extremely difficult. Stop by your local pet store and they will show you what you will need.

You will also need a steel comb, a slicker brush, a sharp pair of barber scissors and a toenail trimmer. Be sure that your scissors are sharp, as a dull pair will be difficult to use and will not do a neat job. You will also need electric clippers with a #15 (or #30 or #40) blade for close work and a #5 blade for clipping the body.

The Bedlington Terrier Club recommends the following for a Utility (non-show) trim. Put your dog on the grooming table and thoroughly comb out the entire dog. Look at a picture of a groomed Bedlington and try to envision your dog in the proper clip.

After your dog is combed out, pick up your clipper and, with the finer (#15) blade, clip the dog's ears, leaving a little tuft at the bottom of the ears. Then, clip the face, throat, tuck-up, belly and tail. (*Note:* Cutting against the direction of the hair growth gives a more even and shorter trim.)

Next, with your #5 blade, clip the back of the hind legs, stopping about three inches above the hock joint where the leg begins to get thicker. Continue with the #5 blade and clip the front edge of the thighs, the tail root, the whole back, but not the brisket, to below the widest part of the ribs.

Continue to clip the chest and shoulders down to the elbows. The throat and sides of the neck will be trimmed to below the base of the ears, but leave a strip like a horse's mane down the back of the neck. Comb out the hair on the legs, brisket, head and neck, and, with your scissors, cut the long hair so that it blends into the clipped areas. Cut the hair shorter on the back of the neck, the elbows and the side of the body. Trim the hair on the feet and legs, and, of course, trim the toenails with your toenail clipper.

Remember, this will be a bit tricky the first few times you do it, but with each grooming, you

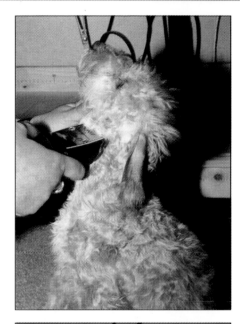

The neck should be closely trimmed.

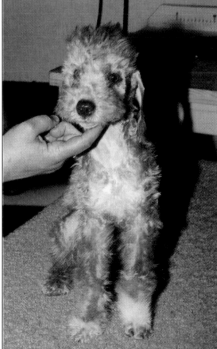

The neck after trimming.

SOAP IT UP

The use of human soap products like shampoo, bubble bath and hand soap can be damaging to a dog's coat and skin. Human products are too strong; they remove the protective oils coating the dog's hair and skin that make him water-resistant. Use only shampoo made especially for dogs. You may like to use a medicated shampoo, which will help to keep external parasites at bay.

challenge of learning to groom and it gives you some quality time with your pet.

BATHING

Dogs do not need to be bathed as often as humans, but occasional bathing is essential for healthy skin and a healthy, shiny coat. Again, like most anything, if you accustom your pup to being bathed as a puppy, it will be second nature by the time he grows up. You want your dog to be at ease in the bath or else it could end up a wet, soapy, messy ordeal for both of you!

Brush your Bedlington Terrier thoroughly before wetting his coat. This will get rid of most

will become more experienced. I grew up with a Wire Fox Terrier, which my mother learned to groom by herself. The dog always looked like a proper Wire Fox Terrier even though she was never trimmed to the extent that a show dog would be. After a few experiences of grooming, you and your dog will walk down the street and passers-by will say, 'Look, that dog looks like a lamb!'

You should comb out your dog's coat once a week and give a bath as needed. Your dog will probably need a trimming about every three months and, if you keep up with your grooming, once you have set the grooming pattern you will find that the next grooming will be much easier. Of course, you can always take your dog to a grooming shop to be cleaned up, usually every three months, but you may enjoy the

BATHING BEAUTY

Once you are sure that the dog is thoroughly rinsed, squeeze the excess water out of his coat with your hand and dry him with a heavy towel. You may choose to use a blaster on his coat or just let it dry naturally. In cold weather, never allow your dog outside with a wet coat.

There are 'dry bath' products on the market, which are sprays and powders intended for spot cleaning, that can be used between regular baths if necessary. They are not substitutes for regular baths, but they are easy to use for touch-ups as they do not require rinsing.

NAIL FILING

You can purchase an electric tool to grind down a dog's nails rather than cut them. Some dogs don't seem to mind the electric grinder but will object strongly to nail clippers. Talking it over with your veterinary surgeon will help you make the right choice.

mats and tangles, which are harder to remove when the coat is wet. Make certain that your dog has a good non-slip surface on which to stand. Begin by wetting the dog's coat, checking the water temperature to make sure that it is neither too hot nor too cold. A shower or hose attachment is necessary for thoroughly wetting and rinsing the coat.

Next, apply shampoo to the dog's coat and work it into a good lather. Wash the head last, as you do not want shampoo to drip into the dog's eyes while you are washing the rest of his body. You should use only a shampoo that is made for dogs. Do not use a product made for human hair. Work the shampoo all the way down to the skin. You can use this opportunity to check the skin for any bumps, bites or other abnormalities. Do not neglect any area of the body—get all of the hard-to-reach places.

Once the dog has been thoroughly shampooed, he requires an equally thorough rinsing. Shampoo left in the coat can be irritating to the dog's skin. Protect his eyes from the shampoo by shielding them with your hand and directing the flow of water in the opposite direction. You should also avoid getting water in the ear canal. Be prepared for your dog to shake out his coat— you might want to stand back, but make sure you have a hold on the dog to keep him from running through the house.

Ear Cleaning

The ears should be kept clean with a cotton wipe and ear powder made especially for dogs. Do not probe into the ear canal with a cotton bud, as this can cause injury. Be on the lookout for any signs of infection or ear mite infestation. If your Bedlington Terrier has been shaking his head or scratching at his ears frequently, this usually indicates a problem. If the dog's ears have an unusual odour, this is a sure sign of mite infestation or infection,

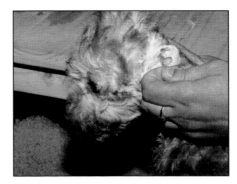

Part of keeping the ears clean is gently removing any excess hairs that grow inside the ears. The hairs can be plucked carefully, using your thumb and forefinger.

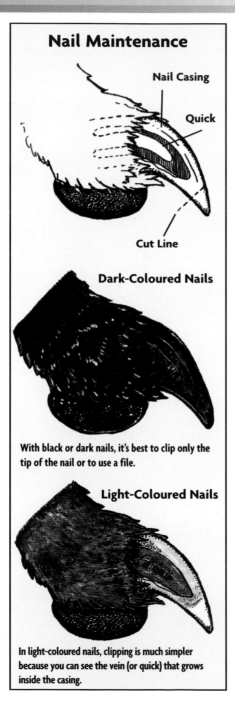

Nail Maintenance

Nail Casing

Quick

Cut Line

Dark-Coloured Nails

With black or dark nails, it's best to clip only the tip of the nail or to use a file.

Light-Coloured Nails

In light-coloured nails, clipping is much simpler because you can see the vein (or quick) that grows inside the casing.

and a signal to have his ears checked by the veterinary surgeon.

Nail Clipping

Your Bedlington Terrier should be accustomed to having his nails trimmed at an early age since nail clipping will be part of your maintenance routine throughout his life. Not only does it look nicer, but long nails can scratch someone unintentionally. Also, a long nail has a better chance of ripping and bleeding, or of causing the feet to spread. A good rule of thumb is that if you can hear your dog's nails clicking on the floor when he walks, his nails are too long.

Before you start cutting, make sure you can identify the 'quick' in each nail. The quick is a blood vessel that runs through the centre of each nail and grows rather close to the end. The quick will bleed if accidentally cut, which will be quite painful for the dog as it contains nerve endings. Keep some type of clotting agent on hand, such as a styptic pencil or styptic powder (the type used for shaving). This will stop the bleeding quickly when applied to the end of the cut nail. Do not panic if you cut the quick, just stop the bleeding and talk soothingly to your dog. Once he has calmed down, move on to the next nail. It is better to clip a little at a time, particularly with black-nailed dogs.

Hold your pup steady as you begin trimming his nails; you do not want him to make any sudden movements or run away. Talk to him soothingly and stroke him as you clip. Holding his foot in your hand, simply take off the end of each nail with one swift clip. You should purchase nail clippers that are made for use on dogs; you can probably find them wherever you buy pet or grooming supplies.

TRAVELLING WITH YOUR DOG

CAR TRAVEL
You should accustom your Bedlington Terrier to riding in a car at an early age. You may or may not take him in the car often, but at the very least he will need to go to the vet and you do not want these trips to be traumatic for the dog or troublesome for you. The safest way for a dog to ride in the car is in his crate. If he uses a crate in the house, you can use the same crate for travel.

Put the pup in the crate and see how he reacts. If he seems uneasy, you can have a passenger hold the pup on his lap while you drive. Another option for car travel is a specially made safety harness for dogs, which straps the dog in much like a seat belt. Do not let the dog roam loose in the vehicle—this is very dangerous! If you should stop short, your dog can be thrown and injured. If the

PEDICURE TIP
A dog that spends a lot of time outside on a hard surface, such as cement or pavement, will have his nails naturally worn down and may not need to have them trimmed as often, except maybe in the colder months when he is not outside as much. Regardless, it is best to get your dog accustomed to the nail-trimming procedure at an early age so that he is used to it. Some dogs are especially sensitive about having their feet touched, but if a dog has experienced it since puppyhood, it should not bother him.

dog starts climbing on you and pestering you while you are driving, you will not be able to concentrate on the road. It is an unsafe situation for everyone— human and canine.

For long trips, be prepared to stop to let the dog relieve himself. Take with you whatever you need to clean up after him, including some paper kitchen towels and perhaps some old towelling for use should he have 'a toileting accident' in the car or suffer from travel sickness.

DID YOU KNOW?
You have a valuable dog. If the dog is lost or stolen, you would undoubtedly become extremely upset. Likewise, if you encounter a lost dog, notify the police or the local animal shelter.

AIR TRAVEL

While it is possible to take a dog on a flight within Britain, this is fairly unusual and advance permission is always required. The dog will be required to travel in a fibreglass crate and you should always check in advance with the airline regarding specific requirements. To help put the dog at ease, give him one of his favourite toys in the crate. Do not feed the dog for at least six hours before the trip in order to minimise his need to relieve himself. However, certain regulations specify that water must always be made available to the dog in the crate.

Make sure your dog is properly identified and that your contact information appears on his ID tags and on his crate. Animals travel in a different area of the plane than human passengers, so every rule must be strictly followed so as to prevent the risk of getting separated from your dog.

BOARDING

So you want to take a family holiday—and you want to include *all* members of the family. You would probably make arrangements for accommodation ahead of time anyway, but this is especially important when travelling with a dog. You do not want to make an overnight stop at the only place around for miles, only to find out that they do not allow dogs. Also, you do not want to reserve a place for your family without confirming that you are travelling with a dog, because, if it is against their policy, you may end up without a place to stay.

Alternatively, if you are travelling and choose not to bring your Bedlington Terrier, you will have to make arrangements for him while you are away. Some options are to take him to a neighbour's house to stay while you are gone,

You should locate a boarding kennel prior to your actually needing it. Meet the staff, see the facilities and discuss such things as costs, feeding, exercise, medical care, etc.

to have a trusted neighbour pop in often or stay at your house or to bring your dog to a reputable boarding kennel. If you choose to board him at a kennel, you should visit in advance to see the facilities provided and where the dogs are kept. Are the dogs' areas spacious and kept clean? Talk to some of the employees and see how they treat the dogs—do they spend time with the dogs, play with them, exercise them, etc.? Also find out the kennel's policy on vaccinations and what they require. This is for all of the dogs' safety, since there is a greater risk of diseases being passed from dog to dog when dogs are kept together.

IDENTIFICATION

Your Bedlington Terrier is your valued companion and friend. That is why you always keep a close eye on him and you have made sure that he cannot escape from the garden or wriggle out of his collar and run away from you. However, accidents can happen and there may come a time when your dog unexpectedly becomes separated from you. If this unfortunate event should occur, the first thing on your mind will be finding him. Proper identification, including an ID tag, a tattoo and possibly a microchip, will increase the chances of his being returned to you safely and quickly.

IDENTIFICATION OPTIONS

As puppies become more and more expensive, especially those puppies of high quality for showing and/or breeding, they have a greater chance of being stolen. The usual collar dog tag is, of course, easily removed. But there are two more permanent techniques that have become widely used for identification.

The puppy microchip implantation involves the injection of a small microchip, about the size of a corn kernel, under the skin of the dog. If your dog shows up at a clinic or shelter, or is offered for resale under less than savoury circumstances, it can be positively identified by the microchip. The microchip is scanned, and a registry quickly identifies you as the owner. This is not only protection against theft, but should the dog run away or go chasing a squirrel and become lost, you have a fair chance of his being returned to you.

Tattooing is done on various parts of the dog, from his belly to his cheeks. The number tattooed can be your telephone number or any other number that you can easily memorise. When professional dog thieves see a tattooed dog, they usually lose interest. Both microchipping and tattooing can be done at your local veterinary clinic. For the safety of our dogs, no laboratory facility or dog broker will accept a tattooed dog as stock.

REAP THE REWARDS

If you start with a normal, healthy dog and give him time, patience and some carefully executed lessons, you will reap the rewards of that training for the life of the dog. And what a life it will be! The two of you will find immeasurable pleasure in the companionship you have built together with love, respect and understanding.

Living with an untrained dog is a lot like owning a piano that you do not know how to play—it is a nice object to look at, but it does not do much more than that to bring you pleasure. Now try taking piano lessons, and suddenly the piano comes alive and brings forth magical sounds and rhythms that set your heart singing and your body swaying.

The same is true with your Bedlington Terrier. Any dog is a big responsibility and, if not trained sensibly, may develop unacceptable behaviour that annoys you or could even cause family friction.

To train your Bedlington Terrier, you may like to enrol in an obedience class. Teach your dog good manners as you learn how and why he behaves the way he does. Find out how to communicate with your dog and how to recognise and understand his communications with you. Suddenly the dog takes on a new role in your life—he is clever, interesting, well behaved and fun to be with. He demonstrates his bond of devotion to you daily. In other words, your Bedlington Terrier does wonders for your ego because he constantly reminds you that you are not only his leader, you are his hero!

Those involved with teaching dog obedience and counselling owners about their dogs' behaviour have discovered some interesting facts about dog ownership. For example, training dogs when they are puppies results in the highest rate of success in developing well-mannered and well-adjusted adult dogs. Training an older dog, from six months to six years of age, can produce almost equal results providing that the owner accepts the dog's slower rate of learning capability and is willing to work patiently to help the dog succeed at developing to his fullest potential. Unfortunately, many owners of untrained adult dogs lack the patience factor, so they do not persist until their dogs are successful at learning particular behaviours.

An intelligent and quick breed, the Bedlington Terrier can be trained to respond to a multitude of commands and tricks...but it doesn't hurt to have a treat on hand!

THE HAND THAT FEEDS

To a dog's way of thinking, your hands are like his mouth in terms of a defence mechanism. If you squeeze him too tightly, he might just bite you because that would be his normal response. This is not aggressive biting and, although all biting should be discouraged, you need the discipline in learning how to handle your dog.

Training a puppy aged 10 to 16 weeks (20 weeks at the most) is like working with a dry sponge in a pool of water. The pup soaks up whatever you show him and constantly looks for more things to do and learn. At this early age, his body is not yet producing hormones, and therein lies the reason for such a high rate of success. Without hormones, he is focused on his owners and not particularly interested in investigating other places, dogs, people, etc. You are his leader: his provider of food, water, shelter and security. He latches onto you and wants to stay close. He will usually follow you from room to room, will not let you out of his sight when you are outdoors with him and will respond in like manner to the people and animals you encounter. If you greet a friend warmly, he will be happy to greet the person as well. If, however, you are hesitant or anxious about the approach of a stranger, he will respond accordingly.

Once the puppy begins to produce hormones, his natural

HONOUR AND OBEY

Dogs are the most honourable animals in existence. They consider another species (humans) as their own. They interface with you. You are their leader. Puppies perceive children to be on their level; their actions around small children are different from their behaviour around their adult masters.

PARENTAL GUIDANCE

Training a dog is a life experience. Many parents admit that much of what they know about raising children they learned from caring for their dogs. Dogs respond to love, fairness and guidance, just as children do. Become a good dog owner and you may become an even better parent.

curiosity emerges and he begins to investigate the world around him. It is at this time when you may notice that the untrained dog begins to wander away from you and even ignore your commands to stay close. When this behaviour becomes a problem, you have two choices: get rid of the dog or train him. It is strongly urged that you choose the latter option.

You usually will be able to find obedience classes within a reasonable distance from your home, but you can also do a lot to train your dog yourself. Sometimes there are classes available, but the tuition is too costly. Whatever the circumstances, the solution to training your dog without obedience classes lies within the pages of this book.

This chapter is devoted to helping you train your Bedlington Terrier at home. If the recommended procedures are

CANINE DEVELOPMENT SCHEDULE

It is important to understand how and at what age a puppy develops into adulthood. If you are a puppy owner, consult the following Canine Development Schedule to determine the stage of development your puppy is currently experiencing. This knowledge will help you as you work with the puppy in the weeks and months ahead.

Period	Age	Characteristics
FIRST TO THIRD	**BIRTH TO SEVEN WEEKS**	Puppy needs food, sleep and warmth, and responds to simple and gentle touching. Needs mother for security and disciplining. Needs littermates for learning and interacting with other dogs. Pup learns to function within a pack and learns pack order of dominance. Begin socialising with adults and children for short periods. Begins to become aware of its environment.
FOURTH	**EIGHT TO TWELVE WEEKS**	Brain is fully developed. Needs socialising with outside world. Remove from mother and littermates. Needs to change from canine pack to human pack. Human dominance necessary. Fear period occurs between 8 and 12 weeks. Avoid fright and pain.
FIFTH	**THIRTEEN TO SIXTEEN WEEKS**	Training and formal obedience should begin. Less association with other dogs, more with people, places, situations. Period will pass easily if you remember this is pup's change-to-adolescence time. Be firm and fair. Flight instinct prominent. Permissiveness and over-disciplining can do permanent damage. Praise for good behaviour.
JUVENILE	**FOUR TO EIGHT MONTHS**	Another fear period about 7 to 8 months of age. It passes quickly, but be cautious of fright and pain. Sexual maturity reached. Dominant traits established. Dog should understand sit, down, come and stay by now.

NOTE: THESE ARE APPROXIMATE TIME FRAMES. ALLOW FOR INDIVIDUAL DIFFERENCES IN PUPPIES.

followed faithfully, you may expect positive results that will prove rewarding both to you and your dog.

Whether your new charge is a puppy or a mature adult, the methods of teaching and the techniques we use in training basic behaviours are the same. After all, no dog, whether puppy or adult, likes harsh or inhumane

TRAINING TIP
Dogs will do anything for your attention. If you reward the dog when he is calm and resting, you will develop a well-mannered dog. If, on the other hand, you greet your dog excitedly and encourage him to wrestle with you, the dog will greet you the same way and you will have a hyperactive dog on your hands.

MEALTIME
Mealtime should be a peaceful time for your puppy. Do not put his food and water bowls in a high-traffic area in the house. For example, give him his own little corner of the kitchen where he can eat undisturbed and where he will not be underfoot. Do not allow small children or other family members to disturb the pup when he is eating.

methods. All creatures, however, respond favourably to gentle motivational methods and sincere praise and encouragement. Now let us get started.

HOUSE-TRAINING
You can train a puppy to relieve himself wherever you choose, but this must be somewhere suitable. You should bear in mind from the outset that when your puppy is old enough to go out in public places, any canine deposits must be removed at once. You will always have to carry with you a small plastic bag or 'poop-scoop.'

Outdoor training includes such surfaces as grass, soil and cement. Indoor training usually means training your dog to newspaper. When deciding on the surface and location that you will want your Bedlington Terrier to use, be sure it is going to be permanent. Training your dog to grass and then changing your mind a few months later is extremely difficult for both dog and owner.

Next, choose the command you will use each and every time you want your puppy to void. 'Hurry up' and 'Toilet' are examples of commands commonly used by dog owners. Get in the habit of giving the puppy your chosen relief command before you take him out. That way, when he becomes an adult, you will be able to determine if he wants to go out when you ask him. A confirmation will be signs of interest: wagging his tail, watching you intently, going to the door, etc.

PUPPY'S NEEDS

Puppy needs to relieve himself after play periods, after each meal,

THINK BEFORE YOU BARK

Dogs are sensitive to their masters' moods and emotions. Use your voice wisely when communicating with your dog. Never raise your voice at your dog unless you are angry and trying to correct him. 'Barking' at your dog can become as meaningless as 'dogspeak' is to you. Think before you bark!

PAPER CAPER

Never line your pup's sleeping area with newspaper. Puppy litters are usually raised on newspaper and, once in your home, the puppy will immediately associate newspaper with voiding. Never put newspaper on any floor while house-training, as this will only confuse the puppy. If you are paper-training him, use paper in his designated relief area ONLY. Finally, restrict water intake after evening meals. Offer a few licks at a time—never let a young puppy gulp water after meals.

after he has been sleeping and at any time he indicates that he is looking for a place to urinate or defecate. The urinary and intestinal tract muscles of very young puppies are not fully developed. Therefore, like human babies, puppies need to relieve themselves frequently.

Take your puppy out often—

every hour for an eight-week-old, for example—and always immediately after sleeping and eating. The older the puppy, the less often he will need to relieve himself. Finally, as a mature healthy adult, he will require only three to five relief trips per day.

HOUSING

Since the types of housing and control you provide for your puppy have a direct relationship on the success of house-training, we consider the various aspects of both before we begin training.

Taking a new puppy home and turning him loose in your house can be compared to turning a child loose in a sports arena and telling the child that the place is all his! The sheer enormity of the

This puppy made it to the door, but the owner didn't get there in time. Your puppy will tell you through his behaviour when it's time to go out—do not ignore the signs!

THE GOLDEN RULE
The golden rule of dog training is simple. For each 'question' (command), there is only one correct answer (reaction). One command = one reaction. Keep practising the command until the dog reacts correctly without hesitating. Be repetitive but not monotonous. Dogs get bored just as people do!

place would be too much for him to handle. Instead, offer the puppy clearly defined areas where he can play, sleep, eat and live. A room of the house where the family gathers is the most obvious choice. Puppies are social animals and need to feel a part of the pack right from the start. Hearing your voice, watching you while you are doing things and smelling you nearby are all positive reinforcers that he is now a member of your pack. Usually a family room, the kitchen or a nearby adjoining breakfast area is ideal for providing safety and security for both puppy and owner.

Within the designated room, there should be a smaller area that the puppy can call his own. An

alcove, a wire or fibreglass dog crate or a fenced (not boarded!) corner from which he can view the activities of his new family will be fine. The size of the area or crate is the key factor here. The area must be large enough so that the puppy can lie down and stretch out, as well as stand up, without rubbing his head on the top. At the same time, it must be small enough so that he cannot relieve himself at one end and sleep at the other without coming into contact with his droppings before he is fully trained to relieve himself outside. Dogs are, by nature, clean animals and will not remain close to their relief areas unless forced to do so. In those cases, they then become dirty dogs and usually remain that way for life.

The dog's designated area should contain clean bedding and a toy. Water must always be available, in a non-spill container.

CONTROL

By control, we mean helping the puppy to create a lifestyle pattern that will be compatible to that of his human pack (YOU!). Just as we guide little children to learn our way of life, we must show the puppy when it is time to play, eat, sleep, exercise and even entertain himself.

Your puppy should always sleep in his crate. He should also learn that, during times of

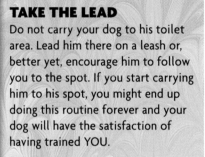

TAKE THE LEAD
Do not carry your dog to his toilet area. Lead him there on a leash or, better yet, encourage him to follow you to the spot. If you start carrying him to his spot, you might end up doing this routine forever and your dog will have the satisfaction of having trained YOU.

household confusion and excessive human activity, such as at breakfast when family members are preparing for the day, he can play by himself in relative safety and comfort in his designated area. Each time you leave the puppy alone, he should understand exactly where he is to stay.

Puppies are chewers. They cannot tell the difference between lamp cords, television wires, shoes, table legs, etc. Chewing into a television wire, for example, can be fatal to the puppy, while a shorted wire can start a

HOW MANY TIMES A DAY?

AGE	RELIEF TRIPS
To 14 weeks	10
14–22 weeks	8
22–32 weeks	6
Adulthood	4
(dog stops growing)	

These are estimates, of course, but they are a guide to the MINIMUM opportunities a dog should have each day to relieve itself.

pup to his designated area not only keeps him safe but also avoids his engaging in destructive behaviours when you are not around.

Times of excitement, such as special occasions, family parties, etc., can be fun for the puppy, providing that he can view the activities from the security of his designated area. He is not underfoot and he is not being fed all sorts of titbits that will probably cause him stomach distress, yet he still feels a part of the fun.

SCHEDULE

A puppy should be taken to his relief area each time he is released from his designated area, after meals, after a play session and when he first awakens in the morning (at age eight weeks, this can mean 5 a.m.!). The puppy will indicate that he's ready 'to go' by

fire in the house. If the puppy chews on the arm of the chair when he is alone, you will probably discipline him angrily when you get home. Thus, he makes the association that your coming home means he is going to be punished. (He will not remember chewing the chair and is incapable of making the associ-ation of the discipline with his naughty deed.) Accustoming the

THE SUCCESS METHOD

Success that comes by luck is usually short-lived. Success that comes by well-thought-out proven methods is often more easily achieved and permanent. This is the Success Method. It is designed to give you, the puppy owner, a simple yet proven way to help your puppy develop clean living habits and a feeling of security in his new environment.

circling or sniffing busily—do not misinterpret these signs. For a puppy less than ten weeks of age, a routine of taking him out every hour is necessary. As the puppy grows, he will be able to wait for longer periods of time.

Keep trips to his relief area short. Stay no more than five or six minutes and then return to the house. If he goes during that time, praise him lavishly and take him indoors immediately. If he does not, but he has an accident when you go back indoors, pick him up immediately, say 'No! No!' and return to his relief area. Wait a few minutes, then return to the house again. Never hit a puppy or rub his face in urine or excrement when he has had an accident!

Once indoors, put the puppy

THE SUCCESS METHOD
6 Steps to Successful Crate Training

1 Tell the puppy 'Crate time!' and place him in the crate with a small treat (a piece of cheese or half of a biscuit). Let him stay in the crate for five minutes while you are in the same room. Then release him and praise lavishly. Never release him when he is fussing. Wait until he is quiet before you let him out.

2 Repeat Step 1 several times a day.

3 The next day, place the puppy in the crate as before. Let him stay there for ten minutes. Do this several times.

4 Continue building time in five-minute increments until the puppy stays in his crate for 30 minutes with you in the room. Always take him to his relief area after prolonged periods in his crate.

5 Now go back to Step 1 and let the puppy stay in his crate for five minutes, this time while you are out of the room.

6 Once again, build crate time in five-minute increments with you out of the room. When the puppy will stay willingly in his crate (he may even fall asleep!) for 30 minutes with you out of the room, he will be ready to stay in it for several hours at a time.

It won't take long for your pup to recognise his chosen spot in the garden. His nose will reliably lead him there time after time.

provide him with undivided attention.

Each time you put your puppy in his own area, use the same command, whatever suits best. Soon he will run to his crate or special area when he hears you say those words.

Crate training provides safety for you, the puppy and the home. It also provides the puppy with a feeling of security, and that helps the puppy achieve self-confidence and clean habits. Remember that one of the primary ingredients in house-training your puppy is control. Regardless of your lifestyle, there will always be occasions when you will need to have a place where your dog can stay and be happy and safe. Crate training is the answer for now and in the future.

In conclusion, a few key

in his crate until you have had time to clean up his accident. Then, release him to the family area and watch him more closely than before. Chances are, his accident was a result of your not picking up his signal or waiting too long before offering him the opportunity to relieve himself. Never hold a grudge against the puppy for accidents.

Let the puppy learn that going outdoors means it is time to relieve himself, not to play. Once trained, he will be able to play indoors and out and still differentiate between the times for play versus the times for relief.

Help him develop regular hours for naps, being alone, playing by himself and just resting, all in his crate. Encourage him to entertain himself while you are busy with your activities. Let him learn that having you near is comforting, but it is not your main purpose in life to

PLAN TO PLAY

The puppy should also have regular play and exercise sessions when he is with you or a family member. Exercise for a very young puppy can consist of a short walk around the house or garden. Playing can include fetching games with a large ball or a special raggy. (All puppies teethe and need soft things upon which to chew.) Remember to restrict play periods to indoors within his living area (the family room, for example) until he is completely house-trained.

CONSISTENCY PAYS OFF

Dogs need consistency in their feeding schedule, exercise and toilet breaks, and in the verbal commands you use. If you use 'Stay' on Monday and 'Stay here, please' on Tuesday, you will confuse your dog. Don't demand perfect behaviour during training classes and then let him have the run of the house the rest of the day. Above all, lavish praise on your pet consistently every time he does something right. The more he feels he is pleasing you, the more willing he will be to learn.

elements are really all you need for a successful house-training method—consistency, frequency, praise, control and supervision. By following these procedures with a normal, healthy puppy, you and the puppy will soon be past the stage of accidents and ready to move on to a full and rewarding life together.

ROLES OF DISCIPLINE, REWARD AND PUNISHMENT

Discipline, training one to act in accordance with rules, brings order to life. It is as simple as that. Without discipline, particularly in a group society, chaos will reign supreme and the group will eventually perish. Humans and canines are social animals and need some form of discipline in order to function effectively. They must procure food, protect their home base and their young and reproduce to keep their species going. If there were no discipline in the lives of social animals, they would eventually die from starvation and/or predation by other stronger animals.

In the case of domestic canines, discipline in their lives is needed in order for them to understand how their pack (you and other family members) functions and how they must act in order to survive.

A large humane society in a highly populated area recently surveyed dog owners regarding their satisfaction with their relationships with their dogs. People who had trained their dogs were 75% more satisfied with their pets than those who had never trained their dogs.

Dr Edward Thorndike, a psychologist, established *Thorndike's Theory of Learning*, which states that a behaviour that results in a pleasant event tends to be repeated. A behaviour that

Always clean up after your Bedlington has relieved itself, whether in your own garden or in a public place.

KEEP SMILING

Never train your dog, puppy or adult, when you are angry or in a sour mood. Dogs are very sensitive to human feelings, especially anger, and if your dog senses that you are angry or upset, he will connect your anger with his training and learn to resent or fear his training sessions.

likely to do it again because he enjoyed the end result.

Occasionally, punishment, a penalty inflicted for an offence, is necessary. The best type of punishment often comes from an outside source. For example, a child is told not to touch the stove because he may get burned. He disobeys and touches the stove. In doing so, he receives a burn. From that time on, he respects the heat of the stove and avoids contact with it. Therefore, a behaviour that results in an unpleasant event tends not to be repeated.

A good example of a dog learning the hard way is the dog who chases the house cat. He is told many times to leave the cat alone, yet he persists in teasing the cat. Then, one day, the dog begins chasing the cat but the cat turns and swipes a claw across the dog's face, leaving the dog with a painful gash on his nose. The final result is that the dog stops chasing the cat. Again, a behaviour that results in an unpleasant event tends not to be repeated.

TRAINING EQUIPMENT

COLLAR AND LEAD

For a Bedlington Terrier, the collar and lead that you use for training must be one with which you are easily able to work, not too heavy for the dog and perfectly safe.

results in an unpleasant event tends not to be repeated. It is this theory upon which training methods are based today. For example, if you manipulate a dog to perform a specific behaviour and reward him for doing it, he is

TREATS

Have a bag of treats on hand; something nutritious and easy to swallow works best. Use a soft treat, a chunk of cheese or a piece of cooked chicken rather than a dry biscuit. By the time the dog has finished chewing a dry treat, he will forget why he is being rewarded in the first place!

Using food rewards will not teach a dog to beg at the table— the only way to teach a dog to beg at the table is to give him food from the table. In training, rewarding the dog with a food treat will help him associate praise and the treats with learning new behaviours that obviously please his owner.

Crates made of wire are popular for use in the home. With a Bedlington, who loves to be part of the action, the open wire allows him to see all that's going on around him.

TRAINING BEGINS: ASK THE DOG A QUESTION

In order to teach your dog anything, you must first get his attention. After all, he cannot learn anything if he is looking away from you with his mind on something else.

To get your dog's attention,

OPEN MINDS

Dogs are as different from each other as people are. What works for one dog may not work for another. Have an open mind. If one method of training is unsuccessful, try another.

COMMAND STANCE

Stand up straight and authoritatively when giving your dog commands. Do not issue commands when lying on the floor or lying on your back on the sofa. If you are on your hands and knees when you give a command, your dog will think you are positioning yourself to play.

ask him 'School?', and immediately walk over to him and give him a treat as you tell him 'Good dog.' Wait a minute or two and repeat the routine, this time with a treat in your hand as you approach within a foot of the dog. Do not go directly to him, but stop about a foot short of him and hold out the treat as you ask 'School?' He will see you approaching with a treat in your hand and most likely begin walking toward you. As you meet, give him the treat and praise again.

The third time, ask the question, have a treat in your hand and walk only a short distance toward the dog so that he must walk almost all the way to you. As he reaches you, give him the treat and praise again.

By this time, the dog will probably be getting the idea that if he pays attention to you, especially when you ask that question, it will pay off in treats and enjoyable activities for him. In other words, he learns that 'school' means doing great things with you that are fun and that result in positive attention for him.

Remember that the dog does not understand your verbal language; he only recognises sounds. Your question translates to a series of sounds for him, and those sounds become the signal to go to you and pay attention. The dog learns that if he does this, he will get to interact with you plus receive treats and praise.

THE BASIC COMMANDS

TEACHING SIT

Now that you have the dog's attention, attach his lead and hold it in your left hand, and hold a food treat in your right hand. Place your food hand at the dog's nose and let him lick the treat but not take it from you. Say 'Sit' and slowly raise your food hand from in front of the dog's nose up over his head so that he is looking at the ceiling. As he bends his head upward, he will have to bend his knees to maintain his balance. As he bends his knees, he will assume a sit position. At that point, release the food treat and praise lavishly with comments such as 'Good dog! Good sit!,' etc. Remember to always praise enthusiastically, because dogs relish verbal praise from their owners and feel so proud of themselves whenever they accomplish a behaviour.

You should have no problem teaching your Bedlington to sit. This basic command is one of the first that every dog learns.

You will not use food forever in getting the dog to obey your commands. Food is only used to teach new behaviours and, once the dog knows what you want when you give a specific command, you will wean him off the food treats but still maintain the verbal praise. After all, you will always have your voice with you, and there will be many times when you have no food rewards but expect the dog to obey.

TEACHING DOWN

Teaching the down exercise is easy when you understand how

DOUBLE JEOPARDY
A dog in jeopardy never lies down. He stays alert on his feet because instinct tells him that he may have to run away or fight for his survival. Therefore, if a dog feels threatened or anxious, he will not lie down. Consequently, it is important to have the dog calm and relaxed as he learns the down exercise.

the dog perceives the down position, and it is very difficult when you do not. Dogs perceive the down position as a submissive one; therefore, teaching the down exercise by using a forceful method can sometimes make the dog develop such a fear of the down that he either runs away when you say 'Down' or he attempts to snap at the person who tries to force him down.

Have the dog sit close alongside your left leg, facing in the same direction as you are.

Hold the lead in your left hand and a food treat in your right. Now place your left hand lightly on the top of the dog's shoulders where they meet above the spinal cord. Do not push down on the dog's shoulders; simply rest your left hand there so you can guide the dog to lie down close to your left leg rather than to swing away from your side when he drops.

Now place the food hand at the dog's nose, say 'Down' very softly (almost a whisper), and slowly lower the food hand to the dog's front feet. When the food hand reaches the floor, begin moving it forward along the floor in front of the dog. Keep talking softly to the dog, saying things like, 'Do you want this treat? You can do this, good dog.' Your reassuring tone of voice will help calm the dog as he tries to follow the food hand in order to get the treat.

When the dog's elbows touch the floor, release the food and praise softly. Try to get the dog to maintain that down position for several seconds before you let him sit up again. The goal here is to get the dog to settle down and not feel threatened in the down position.

TEACHING STAY

It is easy to teach the dog to stay in either a sit or a down position. Again, we use food and praise during the teaching process as we help the dog to understand exactly what it is that we are expecting him to do.

To teach the sit/stay, start with the dog sitting on your left side as before and hold the lead in your left hand. Have a food treat in your right hand and place your food hand at the dog's nose. Say 'Stay' and step out on your right foot to stand directly in front of the dog, toe to toe, as he licks and nibbles the treat. Be sure to keep his head facing upward to maintain the sit position. Count to five and then swing around to stand next to the dog again with him on your left. As soon as you get back to the original position, release the food and praise lavishly.

To teach the down/stay, do the down as previously described. As soon as the dog lies down, say 'Stay' and step out on your right foot just as you did in the sit/stay. Count to five and then return to stand beside the dog with him on your left side. Release the treat and praise as always.

Within a week or ten days, you can begin to add a bit of distance between you and your dog when you leave him. When you do, use your left hand open with the palm facing the dog as a stay signal, much the same as the hand signal a constable uses to stop traffic at an intersection. Hold the food treat in your right hand as before, but this time the food will not be touching the dog's nose. He will watch the food hand and quickly learn that he is going to get that treat as soon as you return to his side.

When you can stand 1 metre away from your dog for 30 seconds, you can then begin building time and distance in both

'NO' MEANS 'NO!'

Dogs do not understand our language. They can be trained to react to a certain sound, at a certain volume. If you say 'No, Oliver' in a very soft pleasant voice it will not have the same meaning as 'No, Oliver!!' when you shout it as loud as you can. You should never use the dog's name during a reprimand, just the command NO!!

Since dogs don't understand words, comics often use dogs trained with opposite meanings. Thus, when the comic commands his dog to SIT the dog will stand up, and vice versa.

call him to you. Always praise lavishly when he stays.

TEACHING COME

If you make teaching 'come' an exciting experience, you should never have a 'student' that does not love the game or that fails to come when called. The secret, it seems, is never to teach the word 'come.'

At times when an owner most wants his dog to come when called, the owner is likely to be upset or anxious and he allows these feelings to come through in the tone of his voice when he calls his dog. Hearing that desperation in his owner's voice, the dog fears the results of going to him and therefore either disobeys outright or runs in the opposite direction. The secret, therefore, is to teach the dog a game and, when you want him to come to you, simply play the game. It is practically a no-fail solution!

To begin, have several members of your family take a few food treats and each go into a different room in the house. Everyone takes turns calling the dog, and each person should celebrate the dog's finding him with a treat and lots of happy praise. When a person calls the dog, he is actually inviting the dog to find him and to get a treat as a reward for 'winning.'

A few turns of the 'Where are you?' game and the dog will

FEAR AGGRESSION

Pups who are subjected to physical abuse during training commonly end up with behavioural problems as adults. One common result of abuse is fear aggression, in which a dog will lash out, bare his teeth, snarl and finally bite someone by whom he feels threatened. For example, your daughter may be playing with the dog one afternoon. As they play hide-and-seek, she backs the dog into a corner and, as she attempts to tease him playfully, he bites her hand. Examine the cause of this behaviour. Did your daughter ever hit the dog? Did someone who resembles your daughter hit or scream at the dog?

Fortunately, fear aggression is relatively easy to correct. Have your daughter engage in only positive activities with the dog, such as feeding, petting and walking. She should not give any corrections or negative feedback. If the dog still growls or cowers away from her, allow someone else to accompany them. After approximately one week, the dog should feel that he can rely on her for many positive things, and he will also be prevented from reacting fearfully towards anyone who might resemble her.

stays. Eventually, the dog can be expected to remain in the stay position for prolonged periods of time until you return to him or

'COME' . . . BACK

Never call your dog to come to you for a correction or scold him when he reaches you. That is the quickest way to turn a 'Come' command into 'Go away fast!' Dogs think only in the present tense, and your dog will connect the scolding with coming to you, not with the misbehaviour of a few moments earlier.

behind a bed or under a table. The dog needs to work a little bit harder to find these hiding places, but, when he does, he loves to celebrate with a treat and a tussle with a favourite youngster.

TEACHING HEEL

Heeling means that the dog walks beside the owner without pulling. It takes time and patience on the

understand that everyone is playing the game and that each person has a big celebration awaiting the dog's success at locating him or her. Once the dog learns to love the game, simply calling out 'Where are you?' will bring him running from wherever he is when he hears that all-important question.

The come command is recognised as one of the most important things to teach a dog, but there are trainers who work with thousands of dogs and never teach the actual word 'Come.' Yet these dogs will race to respond to a person who uses the dog's name followed by 'Where are you?' For example, a woman has a 12-year-old companion dog who went blind, but who never fails to locate her owner when asked, 'Where are you?'

Children, in particular, love to play this game with their dogs. Children can hide in smaller places like a shower or bath,

'WHERE ARE YOU?'

When calling the dog, do not say 'Come.' Say things like, 'Rover, where are you? See if you can find me! I have a biscuit for you!' Keep up a constant line of chatter with coaxing sounds and frequent questions such as, 'Where are you?' The dog will learn to follow the sound of your voice to locate you and receive his reward.

HEELING WELL
Teach your dog to HEEL in an enclosed area. Once you think the dog will obey reliably and you want to attempt advanced obedience exercises such as off-lead heeling, test him in a fenced-in area so he cannot run away.

loop end of the lead to your right hand, but keep your left hand short on the lead so that it keeps the dog in close next to you.

Say 'Heel' and step forward on your left foot. Keep the dog close to you and take three steps. Stop and have the dog sit next to you in what we now call the 'heel position.' Praise verbally, but do not touch the dog. Hesitate a moment and begin again with 'Heel,' taking three steps and stopping, at which point the dog is told to sit again.

Your goal here is to have the dog walk those three steps without pulling on the lead. Once he will walk calmly beside you for three steps without pulling, increase the number of steps you take to five. When he will walk politely beside you while you take five steps, you can increase the length of your walk to ten steps. Keep increasing the length of your stroll until the dog will walk quietly beside you without pulling as long as you want him to heel. When you stop heeling, indicate to the dog that the exercise is over by verbally

owner's part to succeed at teaching the dog that he (the owner) will not proceed unless the dog is walking calmly beside him. Neither pulling out ahead on the lead nor lagging behind is acceptable.

Begin by holding the lead in your left hand as the dog sits beside your left leg. Move the

TRAINING TIP
If you are walking your dog and he suddenly stops and looks straight into your eyes, ignore him. Pull the leash and lead him into the direction you want to walk.

TUG OF WALK?
If you begin teaching the heel by taking long walks and letting the dog pull you along, he misinterprets this action as an acceptable form of taking a walk. When you pull back on the lead to counteract his pulling, he reads that tug as a signal to pull even harder!

praising as you pet him and say, 'OK, good dog.' The 'OK' is used as a release word, meaning that the exercise is finished and the dog is free to relax.

If you are dealing with a dog who insists on pulling you around, simply 'put on your brakes' and stand your ground until the dog realises that the two of you are not going anywhere until he is beside you and moving at your pace, not his. It may take some time just standing there to convince the dog that you are the leader and that you will be the one to decide on the direction and speed of your travel.

Each time the dog looks up at you or slows down to give a slack lead between the two of you, quietly praise him and say, 'Good heel. Good dog.' Eventually, the dog will begin to respond and within a few days he will be walking politely beside you without pulling on the lead. At first, the training sessions should

be kept short and very positive; soon the dog will be able to walk nicely with you for increasingly longer distances. Remember also to give the dog free time and the opportunity to run and play when you have finished heel practice.

WEANING OFF FOOD IN TRAINING
Food is used in training new behaviours. Once the dog understands what behaviour goes with a specific command, it is time to start weaning him off the food treats. At first, give a treat after each exercise. Then, start to give a treat only after every other exercise. Mix up the times when you offer a food reward and the times when you only offer praise so that the dog will never know when he is going to receive both food and praise and when he is

Heeling is basic 'good manners' for all dogs, pet or show. This show dog must heel next to his handler as the judge evaluates his gait.

going to receive only praise. This is called a variable ratio reward system. It proves successful because there is always the chance that the owner will produce a treat, so the dog never stops trying for that reward. No matter what, ALWAYS give verbal praise.

OBEDIENCE CLASSES

It is a good idea to enrol in an obedience class if one is available in your area. If yours is a show dog, ringcraft classes would be more appropriate. Many areas have dog clubs that offer basic obedience training as well as preparatory classes for obedience competition. There are also local dog trainers who offer similar classes.

At obedience shows, dogs can earn titles at various levels of competition. The beginning levels of obedience competition include basic behaviours such as sit, down, heel, etc. The more advanced levels of competition include jumping, retrieving, scent discrimination and signal work. The advanced levels require a dog and owner to put a lot of time and effort into their training. The titles that can be earned at these levels of competition are very prestigious.

OTHER ACTIVITIES FOR LIFE

Whether a dog is trained in the structured environment of a class or alone with his owner at home, there are many activities that can bring fun and rewards to both owner and dog once they have mastered basic control.

Teaching the dog to help out around the home, in the garden or on the farm provides great satisfaction to both dog and owner. In addition, the dog's help makes life a little easier for his owner and raises his stature as a valued companion to his family. It helps give the dog a purpose by occupying his mind and providing an outlet for his energy.

If you are interested in participating in organised competition with your Bedlington Terrier, there are activities other than obedience in which you and your dog can become involved. Going-to-ground activities are every Bedlington's favourite outing, and owners should investigate earth trials sponsored by local terrier clubs. In the US, the American Working Terrier Association was founded in 1971 to encourage and preserve the natural instinct of earth terriers. The dogs are to enter an underground tunnel and to react in a positive manner when facing the quarry. A Working Certificate is issued to dogs who qualify for working in a natural den. The AWTC issues Working, Hunting and Gameness Certificates.

Agility is a popular sport in which dogs run through an

obstacle course that includes various jumps, tunnels and other exercises to test the dog's speed and co-ordination. Mini-agility has been devised by The Kennel Club for small breeds. The events are essentially the same, except all obstacles have been reduced in size so that small dogs can participate. The owners run beside their dogs to give commands and to guide them through the course. Although competitive, the focus is on fun— it's fun to do, fun to watch and great exercise.

Flyball, which began as an American sport in California in the 1970s, has become popular in some canine circles, and some Bedlingtons have applied their lithe bodies to the sport and won titles. In effect, flyball is a relay race where four dogs jump over hurdles and then trigger a ball from a box, catch the ball, and then 'fly' back over the hurdles. It is entertaining for dog and owner and is growing in popularity every year.

Bedlingtons are agile, active, intelligent and ready to participate in most anything— a winning combination that makes him well suited to agility training.

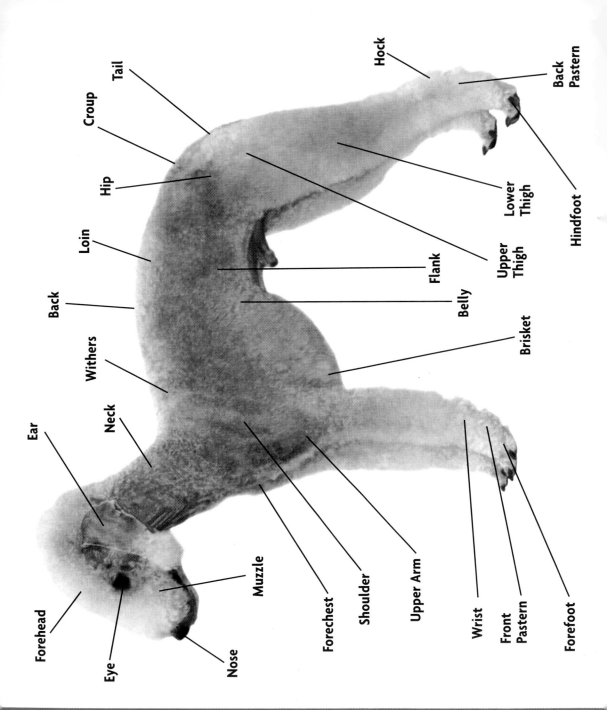

Hock

Back
Pastern

Tail

Croup

Hip

Lower
Thigh

Hindfoot

Loin

Flank

Upper
Thigh

Back

Belly

Withers

Brisket

Neck

Ear

Muzzle

Forehead

Forechest

Shoulder

Upper Arm

Wrist

Front
Pastern

Forefoot

Eye

Nose

PHYSICAL STRUCTURE OF THE BEDLINGTON TERRIER

Dogs suffer from many of the same physical illnesses as people. They might even share many of the same psychological problems. Since people usually know more about human diseases than canine maladies, many of the terms used in this chapter will be familiar but not necessarily those used by veterinary surgeons. We will use the term *x-ray*, instead of the more acceptable term *radiograph*. We will also use the familiar term *symptoms* even though dogs don't have symptoms, which are verbal descriptions of the patient's feelings; dogs have *clinical signs*. Since dogs can't speak, we have to look for clinical signs...but we still use the term *symptoms* in this book.

As a general rule, medicine is *practised*. That term is not arbitrary. Medicine is a constantly changing art as we learn more and more about genetics, electronic aids (like CAT scans) and daily laboratory advances. There are many dog maladies, like canine hip dysplasia, which are not universally treated in the same manner. Some veterinary surgeons opt for surgery more often than others do.

SELECTING A VETERINARY SURGEON

Your selection of a veterinary surgeon should not be based upon personality (as most are) but upon his convenience to your home. You want a vet who is close because you might have emergencies or need to make multiple visits for treatments. You want a vet who has services that you might require such as tattooing and grooming, as well as sophisticated pet supplies and a good reputation for ability and responsiveness. There is nothing more frustrating than having to wait a day or more to get a response from your veterinary surgeon.

All veterinary surgeons are licensed and their diplomas and/or certificates should be displayed in their waiting rooms. There are, however, many veterinary specialities that usually require further studies and internships. There are specialists in heart problems (veterinary cardiologists), skin problems (veterinary dermatologists), teeth and gum problems (veterinary dentists), eye problems (veterinary ophthalmologists) and x-rays (veterinary radiologists), as well

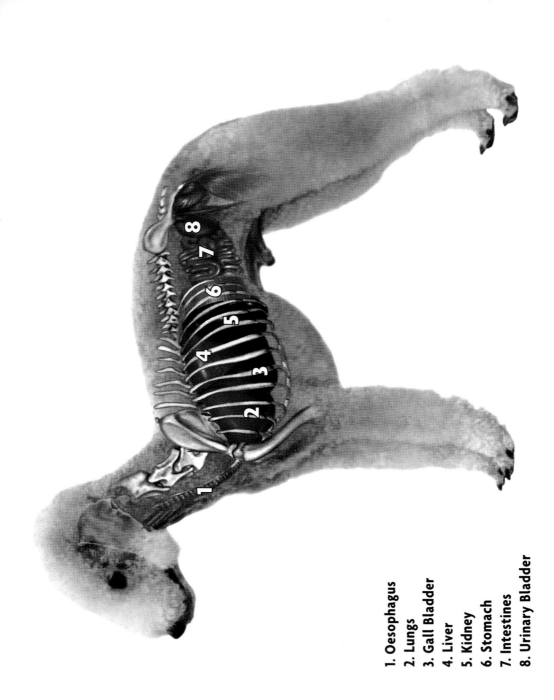

1. Oesophagus
2. Lungs
3. Gall Bladder
4. Liver
5. Kidney
6. Stomach
7. Intestines
8. Urinary Bladder

INTERNAL ORGANS OF THE BEDLINGTON TERRIER

as vets who have specialities in bones, muscles or other organs. Most veterinary surgeons do routine surgery such as neutering, stitching up wounds and docking tails for those breeds in which such is required for show purposes.

When the problem affecting your dog is serious, it is not unusual or impudent to get another medical opinion, although in Britain you are obliged to advise the vets concerned about this. You might also want to compare costs among several veterinary surgeons. Sophisticated health care and veterinary services can be very costly. It is not infrequent that important decisions are based upon financial considerations.

PREVENTATIVE MEDICINE

It is much easier, less costly and more effective to practise preventative medicine than to fight bouts of illness and disease. Properly bred puppies come from parents who were selected based upon

> **DID YOU KNOW?**
> Male dogs are neutered. The operation removes the testicles and requires that the dog be anaesthetised. Recovery takes about one week. Females are spayed. This is major surgery and it usually takes a bitch two weeks to recover.

Breakdown of Veterinary Income by Category

2%	Dentistry
4%	Radiology
12%	Surgery
15%	Vaccinations
19%	Laboratory
23%	Examinations
25%	Medicines

their genetic disease profiles. Their mothers should have been vaccinated, free of all internal and external parasites and properly nourished. The dam can pass on disease resistance to her puppies, which can last for eight to ten weeks, but she can also pass on parasites and many infections. For these reasons, a visit to the veterinary surgeon who cared for the dam is recommended.

A typical American vet's income categorised according to services performed. This survey dealt with small-animal (pets) practices.

VACCINATION SCHEDULING

Most vaccinations are given by injection and should only be done by a veterinary surgeon. Both he and you should keep records of the date of the injection, the identification of the vaccine and the amount given. Some vets give a first vaccination at eight weeks, but most dog breeders prefer the course not to commence until about ten weeks to avoid negating

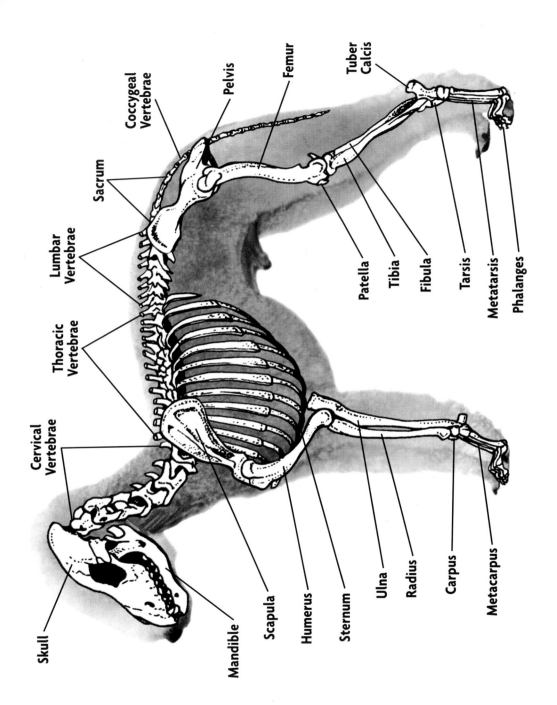

Coccygeal Vertebrae
Pelvis
Femur
Tuber Calcis

Sacrum

Lumbar Vertebrae

Thoracic Vertebrae

Cervical Vertebrae

Patella
Tibia
Fibula
Tarsis
Metatarsis
Phalanges

Skull
Mandible
Scapula
Humerus
Sternum
Ulna
Radius
Carpus
Metacarpus

SKELETAL STRUCTURE OF THE BEDLINGTON TERRIER

any antibodies passed on by the dam. The vaccination scheduling is usually based on a 15-day cycle. You must take your vet's advice regarding when to vaccinate, as this may differ according to the vaccine used. Most vaccinations immunize your puppy against viruses.

The usual vaccines contain immunizing doses of several different viruses such as distemper, parvovirus, parainfluenza and hepatitis, although some veterinary surgeons recommend separate vaccines for each disease. There are other vaccines available when the puppy is at risk. You should rely upon professional advice. This is especially true for the booster-shot programme. Most vaccination programmes require a booster when the puppy is a year old and once a year thereafter. In some cases, circumstances may require more or less frequent immunizations. Kennel cough, more formally known as tracheobronchitis, is treated with a vaccine that is sprayed into the dog's nostrils. Kennel cough is usually included in routine vaccination, but this is often not so effective as for other major diseases.

WEANING TO FIVE MONTHS OLD
Puppies should be weaned by the time they are about two months old. A puppy that remains for at least eight weeks with its mother

BE CAREFUL WHERE YOU WALK YOUR DOG
Dogs who have been exposed to lawns sprayed with herbicides have double and triple the rate of malignant lymphoma. Town dogs are especially at risk, as they are exposed to tailored lawns and gardens. Dogs perspire and absorb through their footpads. Be careful where your dog walks and always avoid any area that appears yellowed from chemical overspray.

and littermates usually adapts better to other dogs and people later in life. Some new owners have their puppies examined by veterinary surgeons immediately, which is a good idea. Vaccination programmes usually begin when the puppy is very young.

The puppy will have its teeth examined, and have its skeletal conformation and general health checked prior to certification by the veterinary surgeon. Puppies in

Normal hairs of a dog enlarged 200 times original size. The cuticle (outer covering) is clean and healthy. Unlike human hair that grows from the base, a dog's hair also grows from the end. Damaged hairs and split ends, illustrated above. Scanning electron micrographs by Dr Dennis Kunkel, University of Hawaii.

certain breeds may have problems with their kneecaps, cataracts and other eye problems, heart murmurs or undescended testicles. They may also have personality problems, and your veterinary surgeon might have training in temperament evaluation.

FIVE TO TWELVE MONTHS OF AGE
Unless you intend to breed or show your dog, neutering the puppy at six months of age is recommended. Discuss this with your veterinary surgeon. Neutering has proven to be extremely beneficial to both male and female puppies. Besides eliminating the possibility of pregnancy, it inhibits (but does not prevent) breast cancer in bitches and prostate cancer in male dogs. Under no circumstances should a bitch be spayed prior to her first season.

Your veterinary surgeon should provide your puppy with a thorough dental evaluation at six

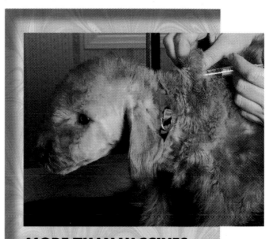

MORE THAN VACCINES
Vaccinations help prevent your new puppy from contracting diseases, but they do not cure them. Proper nutrition as well as parasite control keep your dog healthy and less susceptible to many dangerous diseases. Remember that your dog depends on you to ensure his well-being.

months of age, ascertaining whether all the permanent teeth have erupted properly. A home dental care regimen should be initiated at six months, including brushing weekly and providing good dental devices (such as nylon bones). Regular dental care promotes healthy teeth, fresh breath and a longer life.

ONE TO SEVEN YEARS
Once a year, your grown dog should visit the vet for an examination and vaccination

PUPPY VACCINATIONS
Your veterinary surgeon will probably recommend that your puppy be vaccinated before you take him outside. There are airborne diseases, parasite eggs in the grass and unexpected visits from other dogs that might be dangerous to your puppy's health.

boosters, if needed. Some vets recommend blood tests, a thyroid level check and a dental evaluation to accompany these annual visits. A thorough clinical evaluation by the vet can provide critical background information for your dog. Blood tests are often performed at one year of age, and dental examinations around the third or fourth birthday. In the long run, quality preventative care for your pet can save money, teeth and lives.

SKIN PROBLEMS

Veterinary surgeons are consulted by dog owners for skin problems more than for any other group of diseases or maladies. Dogs' skin is almost as sensitive as human skin, and both suffer from almost the same ailments (though the occurrence of acne in dogs is rare!). For this reason, veterinary dermatology has developed into a speciality practised by many veterinary surgeons.

Since many skin problems have visual symptoms that are almost identical, it requires the skill of an experienced veterinary dermatologist to identify and cure many of the more severe skin disorders. Pet shops sell many treatments for skin problems, but

HEALTH AND VACCINATION SCHEDULE

Age in Weeks:	6TH	8TH	10TH	12TH	14TH	16TH	20-24TH	1 YR
Worm Control	✔	✔	✔	✔	✔	✔	✔	
Neutering								✔
Heartworm		✔		✔		✔	✔	
Parvovirus	✔		✔		✔		✔	✔
Distemper		✔		✔		✔		✔
Hepatitis		✔		✔		✔		✔
Leptospirosis								✔
Parainfluenza	✔		✔		✔			✔
Dental Examination		✔					✔	✔
Complete Physical		✔					✔	✔
Coronavirus				✔			✔	✔
Kennel Cough	✔							
Hip Dysplasia								✔
Rabies							✔	

Vaccinations are not instantly effective. It takes about two weeks for the dog's immune system to develop antibodies. Most vaccinations require annual booster shots. Your veterinary surgeon should guide you in this regard.

most of the treatments are directed at the symptoms and not the underlying problem(s). If your dog is suffering from a skin disorder, you should seek professional assistance as quickly as possible. As with all diseases, the earlier a problem is identified and treated, the more successful is the cure.

HEREDITARY SKIN DISORDERS
Veterinary dermatologists are currently researching a number of skin disorders that are believed to have an hereditary basis. These inherited diseases are transmitted by both parents, who appear (phenotypically) normal but have a recessive gene for the disease, meaning that they carry, but are not affected by, the disease. These diseases pose serious problems to breeders because in some instances there are no methods of identifying carriers. Often the secondary diseases associated with these skin conditions are even more debilitating than the skin disorders themselves, including cancers and respiratory problems; others can be lethal.

Among the hereditary skin disorders, for which the mode of inheritance is known, are acrodermatitis, cutaneous asthenia (Ehlers-Danlos syndrome), sebaceous adenitis, cyclic hematopoiesis, dermatomyositis, IgA deficiency, colour dilution alopaecia and nodular dermatofibrosis. Some of these disorders are limited to one or two breeds, while others affect a large number of breeds. All inherited diseases must be diagnosed and treated by a veterinary specialist.

PARASITE BITES
Many of us are allergic to insect bites. The bites itch, erupt and may even become infected. Dogs have the same reaction to fleas, ticks and/or mites. When an

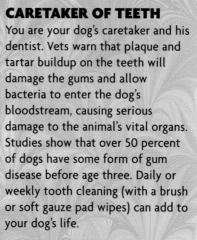

CARETAKER OF TEETH
You are your dog's caretaker and his dentist. Vets warn that plaque and tartar buildup on the teeth will damage the gums and allow bacteria to enter the dog's bloodstream, causing serious damage to the animal's vital organs. Studies show that over 50 percent of dogs have some form of gum disease before age three. Daily or weekly tooth cleaning (with a brush or soft gauze pad wipes) can add to your dog's life.

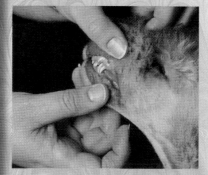

insect lands on you, you have the chance to whisk it away with your hand. Unfortunately, when your dog is bitten by a flea, tick or mite, he can only scratch it away or bite it. By the time the dog has been bitten, the parasite has done some of its damage. It may also have laid eggs, which will cause further problems in the near future. The itching from parasite bites is probably due to the saliva injected into the site when the parasite sucks the dog's blood.

AUTO-IMMUNE SKIN CONDITIONS
An auto-immune skin condition is commonly referred to as a condition in which a person (or dog) is 'allergic' to him- or herself, while an allergy is usually an inflammatory reaction to an outside stimulus. Auto-immune diseases cause serious damage to the tissues that are involved.

The best known auto-immune disease is lupus, which affects people as well as dogs. The symptoms are variable and may affect the kidneys, bones, blood chemistry and skin. It can be fatal to both dogs and humans, though it is not thought to be transmissible. It is usually successfully treated with cortisone, prednisone or a similar corticosteroid, but extensive use of these drugs can have harmful side effects.

AIRBORNE ALLERGIES
An interesting allergy is pollen allergy. Humans have hay fever, rose fever and other fevers from which they suffer during the pollinating season. Many dogs suffer the same allergies. When the pollen count is high, your dog might suffer, but don't expect him to sneeze and have a runny nose like a human would. Dogs react to pollen allergies the same way they react to fleas—they scratch and bite themselves. Dogs, like humans, can be tested for allergens.

FOOD PROBLEMS

FOOD ALLERGIES
Dogs are allergic to many foods that are best-sellers and highly

ACRAL LICK GRANULOMA
Many dogs have a very poorly understood syndrome called acral lick granuloma. The manifestation of the problem is the dog's tireless attack at a specific area of the body, almost always the leg or paw. The dog licks so intensively that he removes the hair and skin, leaving an ugly, large wound. Tiny protuberances, which are outgrowths of new capillaries, bead on the surface of the wound. Owners who notice their dogs' biting and chewing at their extremities should have the vet determine the cause. If lick granuloma is identified, although there is no absolute cure, corticosteroids are the most common treatment.

recommended by breeders and veterinary surgeons. Changing the brand of food that you buy may not eliminate the problem if the element to which the dog is allergic is contained in the new brand.

Recognising a food allergy is difficult. Humans vomit or have rashes when they eat a food to which they are allergic. Dogs neither vomit nor (usually) develop rashes. They react in the same manner as they would to an airborne or flea allergy; they itch, scratch and bite, thus making the diagnosis extremely difficult. While pollen allergies and parasite bites are usually seasonal, food allergies are year-round problems.

FOOD INTOLERANCE

Food intolerance is the inability of the dog to completely digest certain foods. Puppies that may have done very well on their mother's milk may not do well on cow's milk. The results of food intolerance may be evident in loose bowels, passing gas and stomach pains. These are the only obvious symptoms of food intolerance, which makes diagnosis difficult.

TREATING FOOD PROBLEMS

It is possible to handle food allergies and food intolerance yourself. Start by putting your dog on a diet that he has never had. Obviously, if the dog has never eaten this new food, he can't have been allergic or intolerant of it. Start with a single ingredient that is not in the dog's diet at the present time. Ingredients like chopped beef or fish are common in dogs' diets, so try something more exotic like rabbit, pheasant or even just vegetables. Keep the dog on this diet (with no additives) for a month. If the symptoms of food allergy or intolerance disappear, it is quite likely that your dog has a food allergy.

Don't think that the single ingredient cured the problem. You still must find a suitable diet and ascertain which ingredient in the old diet was objectionable. This is most easily done by adding ingredients to the new diet one at a time. Let the dog stay on the modified diet for a month before you add another ingredient. Eventually, you will determine the ingredient that caused the adverse reaction.

An alternative method is to carefully study the ingredients in the diet to which your dog is allergic or intolerant. Identify the main ingredient in this diet and eliminate the main ingredient by buying a different food that does not have that ingredient. Keep experimenting until the symptoms disappear after one month on the new diet.

EXTERNAL PARASITES

FLEAS

Of all the problems to which dogs are prone, none is more well known and frustrating than fleas. Flea infestation is relatively simple to cure but difficult to prevent. Parasites that are harboured inside the body are a bit more difficult to eradicate but they are easier to control.

Magnified head of a dog flea, *Ctenocephalides canis*.

S. E. M. BY DR DENNIS KUNKEL, UNIVERSITY OF HAWAII

To control flea infestation, you have to understand the flea's life cycle. Fleas are often thought of as a summertime problem, but centrally heated homes have changed the patterns and fleas can be found at any time of the year. The most effective method of flea control is a two-stage approach: one stage to kill the adult fleas, and the other to control the development of pre-adult fleas. Unfortunately, no single active ingredient is effective against all stages of the life cycle.

LIFE CYCLE STAGES

During its life, a flea will pass through four life stages: egg, larva, pupa and adult. The adult stage is the most visible and irritating stage of the flea life cycle, and this is

Opposite page: A scanning electron micrograph of a dog or cat flea, *Ctenocephalides*, magnified more than 100x. This image has been colorized for effect.

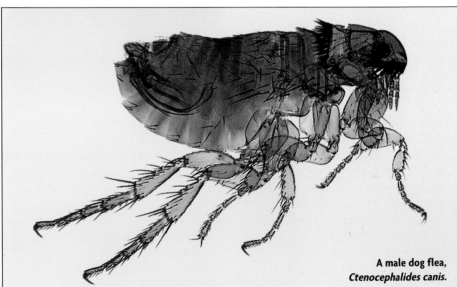

A male dog flea, *Ctenocephalides canis*.

PHOTO BY DR DENNIS KUNKEL, UNIVERSITY OF HAWAII

OPPOSITE: S. E. M. BY DR DENNIS KUNKEL, UNIVERSITY OF HAWAII / PHOTOTAKE

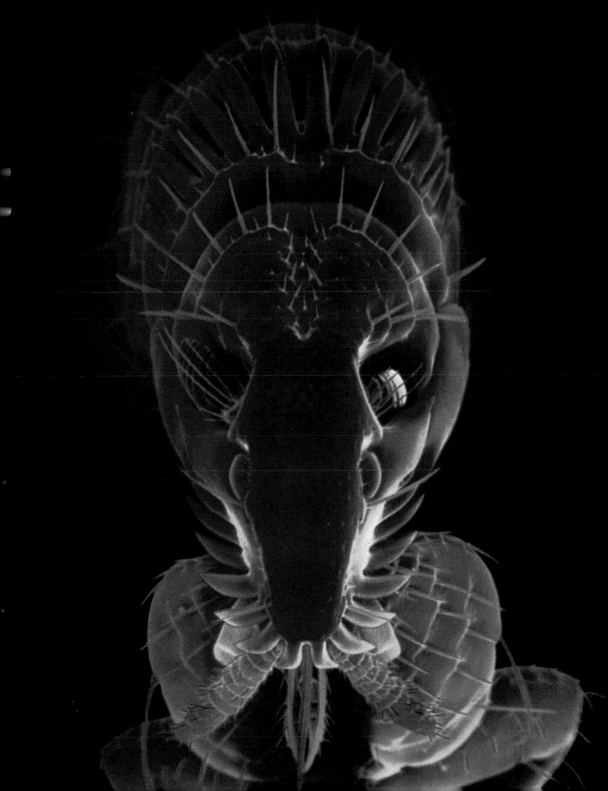

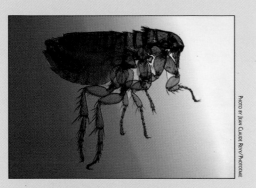

Photo by Jean Claude Revy/Phototake

A LOOK AT FLEAS

Fleas have been around for millions of years and have adapted to changing host animals. They are able to go through a complete life cycle in less than one month or they can extend their lives to almost two years by remaining as pupae or cocoons. They do not need blood or any other food for up to 20 months.

They have been measured as being able to jump 300,000 times and can jump 150 times their length in any direction, including straight up. Those are just a few of the reasons why they are so successful in infesting a dog!

why the majority of flea-control products concentrate on this stage. The fact is that adult fleas account for only 1% of the total flea population, and the other 99% exist in pre-adult stages, i.e. eggs, larvae and pupae. The pre-adult stages are barely visible to the naked eye.

THE LIFE CYCLE OF THE FLEA

Eggs are laid on the dog, usually in quantities of about 20 or 30, several times a day. The female adult flea must have a blood meal before each egg-laying session. When first laid, the eggs will cling to the dog's hair, as the eggs are still moist. However, they will quickly dry out and fall from the dog, especially if the dog moves around or scratches. Many eggs will fall off in the dog's favourite area or an area in which he spends a lot of time, such as his bed.

Once the eggs fall from the dog onto the carpet or furniture, they will hatch into larvae. This takes from one to ten days. Larvae are not particularly mobile and will usually travel only a few inches

The Life Cycle of the Flea

Eggs

Larvae

Pupa

Adult

Photos courtesy of Fleabusters® R_x for fleas.

FLEA KILLERS

Flea-killers are poisonous. You should not spray these toxic chemicals on areas of a dog's body that he licks, on his genitals or on his face. Flea killers taken internally are a better answer, but check with your vet in case internal therapy is not advised for your dog.

INSECT GROWTH REGULATOR (IGR)

Two types of products should be used when treating fleas—a product to treat the pet and a product to treat the home. Adult fleas represent less than 1% of the flea population. The pre-adult fleas (eggs, larvae and pupae) represent more than 99% of the flea population and are found in the environment; it is in the case of pre-adult fleas that products containing an Insect Growth Regulator (IGR) should be used in the home.

IGRs are a new class of compounds used to prevent the development of insects. They do not kill the insect outright, but instead use the insect's biology against it to stop it from completing its growth. Products that contain methoprene are the world's first and leading IGRs. Used to control fleas and other insects, this type of IGR will stop flea larvae from developing and protect the house for up to seven months.

from where they hatch. However, they do have a tendency to move away from light and heavy traffic—under furniture and behind doors are common places to find high quantities of flea larvae.

The flea larvae feed on dead organic matter, including adult flea faeces, until they are ready to change into adult fleas. Fleas will usually remain as larvae for around seven days. After this period, the larvae will pupate into protective pupae. While inside the pupae, the larvae will undergo metamorphosis and change into adult fleas. This can take as little time as a few days, but the adult fleas can remain inside the pupae waiting to hatch for up to two years. The pupae are signalled to hatch by certain stimuli, such as physical pressure—the pupae's being stepped on, heat from an animal lying on the pupae or increased carbon dioxide levels and vibrations—indicating that a suitable host is available.

Once hatched, the adult flea must feed within a few days. Once the adult flea finds a host, it will not leave voluntarily. It only becomes dislodged by grooming or the host animal's scratching. The adult flea will remain on the host for the duration of its life unless forcibly removed.

Photo by Dwight R Kuhn

Dwight R Kuhn's magnificent action photo, showing a flea jumping from a dog's back.

TREATING THE ENVIRONMENT AND THE DOG

Treating fleas should be a two-pronged attack. First, the environment needs to be treated; this includes carpets and furniture, especially the dog's bedding and areas underneath furniture. The environment should be treated with a household spray containing an Insect Growth Regulator (IGR) and an insecticide to kill the adult fleas. Most IGRs are effective against eggs and larvae; they

EN GARDE: CATCHING FLEAS OFF GUARD!

Consider the following ways to arm yourself against fleas:
• Add a small amount of pennyroyal or eucalyptus oil to your dog's bath. These natural remedies repel fleas.
• Supplement your dog's food with fresh garlic (minced or grated) and a hearty amount of brewer's yeast, both of which ward off fleas.
• Use a flea comb on your dog daily. Submerge fleas in a cup of bleach to kill them quickly.
• Confine the dog to only a few rooms to limit the spread of fleas in the home.
• Vacuum daily...and get all of the crevices! Dispose of the bag every few days until the problem is under control.
• Wash your dog's bedding daily. Cover cushions where your dog sleeps with towels, and wash the towels often.

A scanning electron micrograph (S. E. M.) of a dog flea, *Ctenocephalides canis.*

S. E. M. by Dr Dennis Kunkel, University of Hawaii

actually mimic the fleas' own hormones and stop the eggs and larvae from developing into adult fleas. There are currently no treatments available to attack the pupa stage of the life cycle, so the adult insecticide is used to kill the newly hatched adult fleas before they find a host. Most IGRs are active for many months, while adult insecticides are only active for a few days.

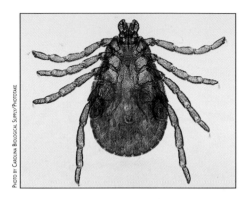

A brown dog tick, *Rhipicephalus sanguineus*, is an uncommon but annoying tick found on dogs.

When treating with a household spray, it is a good idea to vacuum before applying the product. This stimulates as many pupae as possible to hatch into adult fleas. The vacuum cleaner should also be treated with an insecticide to prevent the eggs and larvae that have been hoovered into the vacuum bag from hatching.

An uncommon dog tick of the genus *Ixode*. Magnified 10x.

The second stage of treatment is to apply an adult insecticide to the dog. Traditionally, this would be in the form of a collar or a spray, but more recent innovations include digestible insecticides that poison the fleas when they ingest the dog's blood. Alternatively, there are drops that, when placed on the back of the animal's neck, spread throughout the fur and skin to kill adult fleas.

TICKS AND MITES

Though not as common as fleas, ticks and mites are found all over the tropical and temperate world. They don't bite, like fleas; they harpoon. They dig their sharp proboscis (nose) into the dog's skin and drink the blood. Their only food and drink is dog's blood. Dogs can get Lyme disease, Rocky Mountain spotted fever (normally found in the US only), paralysis and many other diseases from ticks and mites. They may live where fleas are

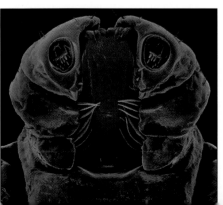

The head of a dog tick, *Dermacentor variabilis*, enlarged and coloured for effect.

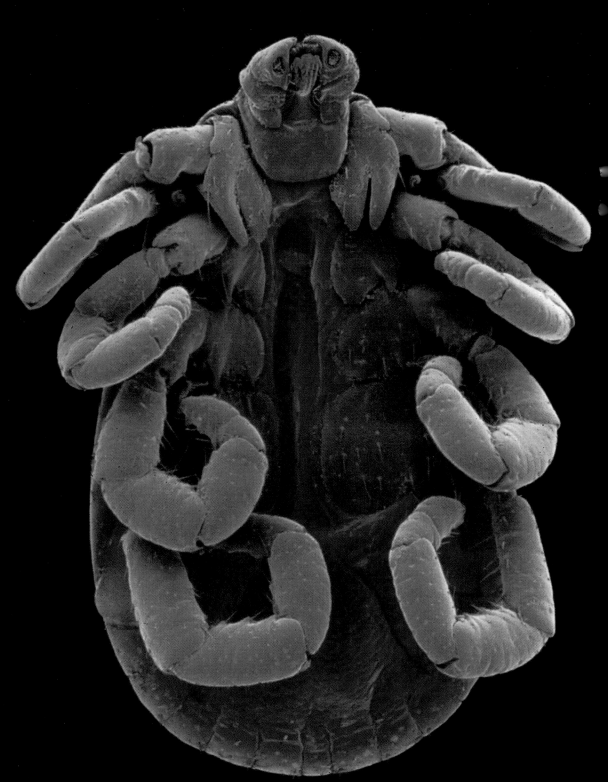

**Human lice look like dog lice;
the two are closely related.**

BEWARE THE DEER TICK

The great outdoors may be fun for your dog, but it also is a home to dangerous ticks. Deer ticks carry a bacterium known as *Borrelia burgdorferi* and are most active in the autumn and spring. When infections are caught early, penicillin and tetracycline are effective antibiotics, but if left untreated the bacteria may cause neurological, kidney and cardiac problems as well as long-term trouble with walking and painful joints.

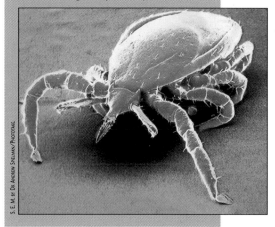

found and they like to hide in cracks or seams in walls wherever dogs live. They are controlled the same way fleas are controlled.

The dog tick, *Dermacentor variabilis*, may well be the most common dog tick in many geographical areas, especially those areas where the climate is hot and humid.

Most dog ticks have life expectancies of a week to six months, depending upon climatic conditions. They can neither jump nor fly, but they

Opposite page:
The dog tick, *Dermacentor variabilis*, is probably the most common tick found on dogs. Look at the strength in its eight legs! No wonder it's hard to detach them.

can crawl slowly and can range up to 5 metres (16 feet) to reach a sleeping or unsuspecting dog.

MANGE

Mites cause a skin irritation called mange. Some are contagious, like *Cheyletiella*, ear mites, scabies and chiggers. Mites that cause ear-mite infestations are usually controlled with Lindane, which can only be

The mange mite, *Psoroptes bovis*.

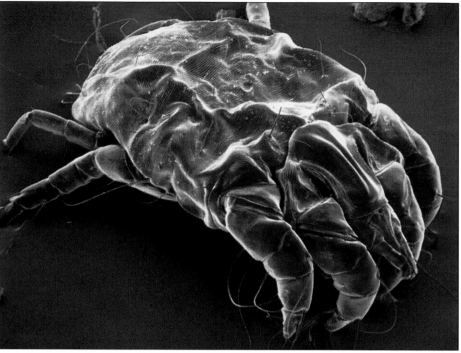

PHOTO BY JAMES HAYDEN-YOAV/PHOTOTAKE

The roundworm, *Rhabditis*. The roundworm can infect both dogs and humans.

PHOTO BY CAROLINA BIOLOGICAL SUPPLY/PHOTOTAKE

The common roundworm, *Ascaris lumbricoides*.

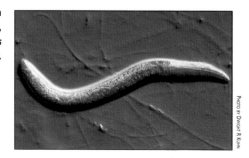

PHOTO BY DWIGHT R KUHN

administered by a vet, followed by Tresaderm at home.

It is essential that your dog be treated for mange as quickly as possible because some forms of mange are transmissible to people.

INTERNAL PARASITES

Most animals—fishes, birds and mammals, including dogs and humans—have worms and other parasites that live inside their bodies. According to Dr Herbert R Axelrod, the fish pathologist, there are two kinds of parasites: dumb and smart. The smart parasites live in peaceful cooperation with their hosts (symbiosis), while the dumb parasites kill their hosts. Most of the worm infections are relatively easy to control. If they are not controlled, they weaken the host dog to the point that other medical problems occur, but they are not dumb parasites.

ROUNDWORMS

The roundworms that infect dogs are scientifically known as *Toxocara canis*. They live in the dog's intestines. The worms shed eggs continually. It has been estimated that a dog produces about 150 grammes of faeces every day. Each gramme of faeces

DEWORMING

Ridding your puppy of worms is *very important* because certain worms that puppies carry, such as tapeworms and roundworms, can infect humans.

Breeders initiate deworming programmes at or about four weeks of age. The routine is repeated every two or three weeks until the puppy is three months old. The breeder from whom you obtained your puppy should provide you with the complete details of the deworming programme.

Your veterinary surgeon can prescribe and monitor the programme of deworming for you. The usual programme is treating the puppy every 15–20 days until the puppy is positively worm-free. It is advised that you only treat your puppy with drugs that are recommended professionally.

ROUNDWORMS

Average size dogs can pass 1,360,000 roundworm eggs every day. For example, if there were only 1 million dogs in the world, the world would be saturated with 1,300 metric tonnes of dog faeces. These faeces would contain 15,000,000,000 roundworm eggs.

Up to 31% of home gardens and children's play boxes in the US contain roundworm eggs.

Flushing dog's faeces down the toilet is not a safe practice because the usual sewage treatments do not destroy roundworm eggs.

Infected puppies start shedding roundworm eggs at 3 weeks of age. They can be infected by their mother's milk.

averages 10,000–12,000 eggs of roundworms. There are no known areas in which dogs roam that do not contain roundworm eggs. The greatest danger of roundworms is that they infect people too! It is wise to have your dog tested regularly for roundworms.

Pigs also have roundworm infections that can be passed to humans and dogs. The typical roundworm parasite is called *Ascaris lumbricoides.*

Left: The roundworm *Rhabditis.* Right: Male and female hookworms. *Ancylostoma caninum* are uncommonly found in pet or show dogs in Britain.

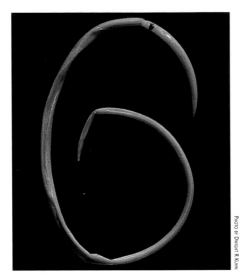

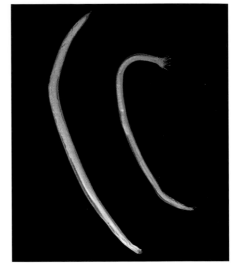

HOOKWORMS

The worm *Ancylostoma caninum* is commonly called the dog hookworm. It is also dangerous to humans and cats. It has teeth by which it attaches itself to the intestines of the dog. It changes the site of its attachment about six times a day and the dog loses blood from each detachment, possibly causing iron-deficiency anaemia. Hookworms are easily purged from the dog with many medications. Milbemycin oxime, which also serves as a heartworm preventative in Collies, can be used for this purpose.

In Britain the 'temperate climate' hookworm (*Uncinaria stenocephala*) is rarely found in pet or show dogs, but can occur in hunting packs, racing Greyhounds and sheepdogs because the worms can be prevalent wherever dogs are exercised regularly on grassland.

TAPEWORMS

There are many species of tapeworm. They are carried by fleas! The dog eats the flea and starts the tapeworm cycle. Humans can also be infected with tapeworms, so don't eat fleas! Fleas are so small that your dog could pass them onto your hands, your plate or your food and thus make it possible for you to ingest a flea that is carrying tapeworm eggs.

The infective stage of the hookworm larva.

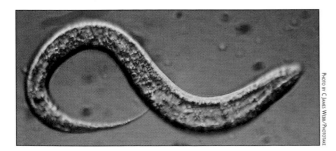

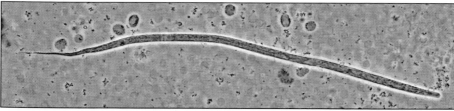

Heartworm,
Dirofilaria immitis.

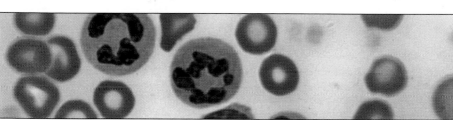

Magnified
heartworm larvae,
Dirofilaria immitis.

While tapeworm infection is not life-threatening in dogs (smart parasite!), it can be the cause of a very serious liver disease for humans. About 50 percent of the humans infected with *Echinococcus multilocularis*, a type of tapeworm that causes alveolar hydatis, perish.

TAPEWORMS

Humans, rats, squirrels, foxes, coyotes, wolves, and domestic dogs are all susceptible to tapeworm infection. Except in humans, tapeworms are usually not a fatal infection. Infected individuals can harbour a thousand parasitic worms.

Tapeworms have two sexes—male and female (many other worms have only one sex—male and female in the same worm).

If dogs eat infected rats or mice, they get the tapeworm disease. One month after attaching to a dog's intestine, the worm starts shedding eggs. These eggs are infective immediately. Infective eggs can live for a few months without a host animal.

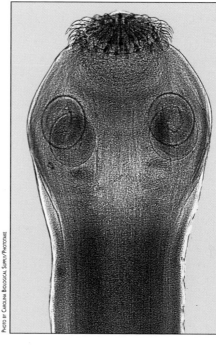

The head and rostellum (the round prominence on the scolex) of a tapeworm, which infects dogs and humans.

The heart of a dog infected with canine heartworm, *Dirofilaria immitis*.

PHOTO BY JAMES E HAYDEN, RPB/PHOTOTAKE

HEARTWORMS

Heartworms are thin, extended worms up to 30 cms (12 ins) long, which live in a dog's heart and the major blood vessels surrounding it. Dogs may have up to 200 worms. Symptoms may be loss of energy, loss of appetite, coughing, the development of a pot belly and anaemia.

Heartworms are transmitted by mosquitoes. The mosquito drinks the blood of an infected dog and takes in larvae with the blood. The larvae, called microfilaria, develop within the body of the mosquito and are passed on to the next dog bitten after the larvae mature. It takes two to three weeks for the larvae to develop to the infective stage within the body of the mosquito. Dogs should be treated at about six weeks of age, and maintained on a prophylactic dose given monthly.

Blood testing for heartworms is not necessarily indicative of how seriously your dog is infected. This is a dangerous disease. Although heartworm is a problem for dogs in America, Australia, Asia and Central Europe, dogs in the United Kingdom are not currently affected by heartworm.

First Aid at a Glance

Burns
Place the affected area under cool water;
use ice if only a small area is burnt.

Bee/Insect bites
Apply ice to relieve swelling;
antihistamine dosed properly.

Animal bites
Clean any bleeding area; apply pressure
until bleeding subsides; go to the vet.

Spider bites
Use cold compress and a pressurised
pack to inhibit venom's spreading.

Antifreeze poisoning
Induce vomiting with hydrogen peroxide.
Seek *immediate* veterinary help!

Fish hooks
Removal best handled by vet;
hook must be cut in order to remove.

Snake bites
Pack ice around bite; contact vet
quickly; identify snake for proper
antivenin.

Car accident
Move dog from roadway with blanket;
seek veterinary aid.

Shock
Calm the dog, keep him warm; seek
immediate veterinary help.

Nosebleed
Apply cold compress to the nose; apply
pressure to any visible abrasion.

Bleeding
Apply pressure above the area; treat
wound by applying a cotton pack.

Heat stroke
Submerge dog in cold bath; cool down
with fresh air and water; go to the vet.

Frostbite/Hypothermia
Warm the dog with a warm bath, electric
blankets or hot water bottles.

Abrasions
Clean the wound and wash out
thoroughly with fresh water;
apply antiseptic.

!! *Remember: an injured dog may attempt
to bite a helping hand from fear and confusion.
Always muzzle the dog before trying to offer assistance.* **!!**

HOMEOPATHY:
an alternative to conventional medicine

'Less is Most'

Using this principle, the strength of a homeopathic remedy is measured by the number of serial dilutions that were undertaken to create it. The greater the number of serial dilutions, the greater the strength of the homeopathic remedy. The potency of a remedy that has been made by making a dilution of 1 part in 100 parts (or 1/100) is 1c or 1cH. If this remedy is subjected to a series of further dilutions, each one being 1/100, a more dilute and stronger remedy is produced. If the remedy is diluted in this way six times, it is called 6c or 6cH. A dilution of 6c is 1 part in 1,000,000,000,000. In general, higher potencies in more frequent doses are better for acute symptoms and lower potencies in more infrequent doses are more useful for chronic, long-standing problems.

CURING OUR DOGS NATURALLY

Holistic medicine means treating the whole animal as a unique, perfect living being. Generally, holistic treatments do not suppress the symptoms that the body naturally produces, as do most medications prescribed by conventional doctors and vets. Holistic methods seek to cure disease by regaining balance and harmony in the patient's environment. Some of these methods include use of nutritional therapy, herbs, flower essences, aromatherapy, acupuncture, massage, chiropractic and, of course, the most popular holistic approach, homeopathy.

Homeopathy is a theory or system of treating illness with small doses of substances which, if administered in larger quantities, would produce the symptoms that the patient already has. This approach is often described as 'like cures like.' Although modern veterinary medicine is geared toward the 'quick fix,' homeopathy relies on the belief that, given the time, the body is able to heal itself and return to its natural, healthy state.

Choosing a remedy to cure a problem in our dogs is the difficult part of homeopathy. Consult with your veterinary surgeon for a professional diagnosis of your dog's symptoms. Often these symptoms require immediate conventional care. If your vet is willing, and knowledgeable, you may attempt a homeopathic remedy. Be aware that cortisone prevents homeopathic remedies from working. There are hundreds of possibilities and combinations to cure many problems in dogs, from basic physical problems such as excessive moulting, fleas or other parasites, obesity, unattractive doggy odour, bad breath, upset tummy, dry, oily or dull coat, diarrhoea, ear problems or eye discharge (including tears and dry or mucousy matter), to behavioural abnormalities, such as fear of loud noises, habitual licking, poor appetite, excessive barking and various phobias. From alumina to zincum metallicum, the remedies span the planet and the imagination…from flowers and weeds to chemicals, insect droppings, diesel smoke and volcanic ash.

Using 'Like to Treat Like'

Unlike conventional medicines that suppress symptoms, homeopathic remedies treat illnesses with small doses of substances that, if administered in larger quantities, would produce the symptoms that the patient already has. While the same homeopathic remedy can be used to treat different symptoms in different dogs, here are some interesting remedies and their uses.

Apis Mellifica
(made from honey bee venom) can be used for allergies or to reduce swelling that occurs in acutely infected kidneys.

Diesel Smoke
can be used to help control travel sickness.

Calcarea Fluorica
(made from calcium fluoride, which helps harden bone structure) can be useful in treating hard lumps in tissues.

Natrum Muriaticum
(made from common salt, sodium chloride) is useful in treating thin, thirsty dogs.

Nitricum Acidum
(made from nitric acid) is used for symptoms you would expect to see from contact with acids, such as lesions, especially where the skin joins the linings of body orifices or openings such as the lips and nostrils.

Symphytum
(made from the herb Knitbone, *Symphytum officianale*) is used to encourage bones to heal.

Urtica Urens
(made from the common stinging nettle) is used in treating painful, irritating rashes.

HOMEOPATHIC REMEDIES FOR YOUR DOG

Symptom/Ailment	Possible Remedy
ALLERGIES	Apis Mellifica 30c, Astacus Fluviatilis 6c, Pulsatilla 30c, Urtica Urens 6c
ALOPAECIA	Alumina 30c, Lycopodium 30c, Sepia 30c, Thallium 6c
ANAL GLANDS (BLOCKED)	Hepar Sulphuris Calcareum 30c, Sanicula 6c, Silicea 6c
ARTHRITIS	Rhus Toxicodendron 6c, Bryonia Alba 6c
CATARACT	Calcarea Carbonica 6c, Conium Maculatum 6c, Phosphorus 30c, Silicea 30c
CONSTIPATION	Alumina 6c, Carbo Vegetabilis 30c, Graphites 6c, Nitricum Acidum 30c, Silicea 6c
COUGHING	Aconitum Napellus 6c, Belladonna 30c, Hyoscyamus Niger 30c, Phosphorus 30c
DIARRHOEA	Arsenicum Album 30c, Aconitum Napellus 6c, Chamomilla 30c, Mercurius Corrosivus 30c
DRY EYE	Zincum Metallicum 30c
EAR PROBLEMS	Aconitum Napellus 30c, Belladonna 30c, Hepar Sulphuris 30c, Tellurium 30c, Psorinum 200c
EYE PROBLEMS	Borax 6c, Aconitum Napellus 30c, Graphites 6c, Staphysagria 6c, Thuja Occidentalis 30c
GLAUCOMA	Aconitum Napellus 30c, Apis Mellifica 6c, Phosphorus 30c
HEAT STROKE	Belladonna 30c, Gelsemium Sempervirens 30c, Sulphur 30c
HICCOUGHS	Cinchona Deficinalis 6c
HIP DYSPLASIA	Colocynthis 6c, Rhus Toxicodendron 6c, Bryonia Alba 6c
INCONTINENCE	Argentum Nitricum 6c, Causticum 30c, Conium Maculatum 30c, Pulsatilla 30c, Sepia 30c
INSECT BITES	Apis Mellifica 30c, Cantharis 30c, Hypericum Perforatum 6c, Urtica Urens 30c
ITCHING	Alumina 30c, Arsenicum Album 30c, Carbo Vegetabilis 30c, Hypericum Perforatum 6c, Mezerium 6c, Sulphur 30c
KENNEL COUGH	Drosera 6c, Ipecacuanha 30c
MASTITIS	Apis Mellifica 30c, Belladonna 30c, Urtica Urens 1m
PATELLAR LUXATION	Gelsemium Sempervirens 6c, Rhus Toxicodendron 6c
PENIS PROBLEMS	Aconitum Napellus 30c, Hepar Sulphuris Calcareum 30c, Pulsatilla 30c, Thuja Occidentalis 6c
PUPPY TEETHING	Calcarea Carbonica 6c, Chamomilla 6c, Phytolacca 6c
TRAVEL SICKNESS	Cocculus 6c, Petroleum 6c

Recognising a Sick Dog

Unlike colicky babies and cranky children, our canine kids cannot tell us when they are feeling ill. Therefore, there are a number of signs that owners can identify to know that their dogs are not feeling well.

Take note for physical manifestations such as:

- unusual, bad odour, including bad breath
- excessive moulting
- wax in the ears, chronic ear irritation
- oily, flaky, dull haircoat
- mucous, tearing or similar discharge in the eyes
- fleas or mites
- mucous in stool, diarrhoea
- sensitivity to petting or handling
- licking at paws, scratching face, etc.

Keep an eye out for behavioural changes as well including:

- lethargy, idleness
- lack of patience or general irritability
- lack of appetite, digestive problems
- phobias (fear of people, loud noises, etc.)
- strange behaviour, suspicion, fear
- coprophagia
- more frequent barking
- whimpering, crying

Get Well Soon

You don't need a DVR or a BVMA to provide good TLC to your sick or recovering dog, but you do need to pay attention to some details that normally wouldn't bother him. The following tips will aid Fido's recovery and get him back on his paws again:

- Keep his space free of irritating smells, like heavy perfumes and air fresheners.
- Rest is the best medicine! Avoid harsh lighting that will prevent your dog from sleeping. Shade him from bright sunlight during the day and dim the lights in the evening.
- Keep the noise level down. Animals are more sensitive to sound when they are sick.

- Be attentive to any necessary temperature adjustments. A dog with a fever needs a cool room and cold liquids. A bitch that is whelping or recovering from surgery will be more comfortable in a warm room, consuming warm liquids and food.
- You wouldn't send a sick child back to school early, so don't rush your dog back into a full routine until he seems absolutely ready.

Number-One Killer Disease in Dogs: CANCER

In every age there is a word associated with a disease or plague that causes humans to shudder. In the 21st century, that word is 'cancer.' Just as cancer is the leading cause of death in humans, it claims nearly half the lives of dogs that die from a natural disease as well as half the dogs that die over the age of ten years.

Described as a genetic disease, cancer becomes a greater risk as the dog ages. Veterinary surgeons and dog owners have become increasingly aware of the threat of cancer to dogs. Statistics reveal that one dog in every five will develop cancer, the most common of which is skin cancer. Many cancers, including prostate, ovarian and breast cancer, can be avoided by spaying and neutering our dogs by the age of six months.

Early detection of cancer can save or extend your dog's life, so it is absolutely vital for owners to have their dogs examined by a qualified veterinary surgeon or oncologist immediately upon detection of any abnormality. Certain dietary guidelines have also proven to reduce the onset and spread of cancer. Foods based on fish rather than beef, due to the presence of Omega-3 fatty acids, are recommended. Other amino acids such as glutamine have significant benefits for canines, particularly those breeds that show a greater susceptibility to cancer.

Cancer management and treatments promise hope for future generations of canines. Since the disease is genetic, breeders should never breed a dog whose parents, grandparents and any related siblings have developed cancer. It is difficult to know whether to exclude an otherwise healthy dog from a breeding programme as the disease does not manifest itself until the dog's senior years.

RECOGNISE CANCER WARNING SIGNS

Since early detection can possibly rescue your dog from becoming a cancer statistic, it is essential for owners to recognise the possible signs and seek the assistance of a qualified professional.

- Abnormal bumps or lumps that continue to grow
- Bleeding or discharge from any body cavity
- Persistent stiffness or lameness
- Recurrent sores or sores that do not heal
- Inappetence
- Breathing difficulties
- Weight loss
- Bad breath or odours
- General malaise and fatigue
- Eating and swallowing problems
- Difficulty urinating and defecating

Disease	Percentage
Cancer	47%
Heart disease	12%
Kidney disease	7%
Epilepsy	4%
Liver disease	4%
Bloat	3%
Diabetes	3%
Stroke	2%
Cushing's disease	2%
Immune diseases	2%
Other causes	14%

The Ten Most Common Fatal Diseases in Pure-bred Dogs

The term *old* is a qualitative term. For dogs, as well as for their masters, old is relative. Certainly we can all distinguish between a puppy Bedlington Terrier and an adult Bedlington Terrier—there are the obvious physical traits, such as size, appearance and coat, and personality traits. Puppies and young dogs like to play with children. Children's natural exuberance is a good match for the seemingly endless energy of young dogs. They like to run, jump, chase and retrieve. When dogs grow older and cease their interaction with children, they are often thought of as being too old to keep pace with the kids. On the other hand, if a Bedlington Terrier is only exposed to older people or quieter lifestyles, his life will normally be less active and the decrease in his activity level as he ages will not be as obvious.

If people live to be 100 years old, dogs live to be 20 years old. While this might seem like a good rule of thumb, it is very inaccurate. When trying to compare dog years to human years, you cannot make a generalisation about all dogs. Terriers as a whole are long-lived dogs and your Bedlington will be no different. If your dog lives to 8 years of age, he will often last until 12 years of age. Give your dog his yearly inoculations, visit the vet as needed, feed him a good diet and give him plenty of exercise and your dog should live a long life with you and give you much pleasure. Average lifespan for many terriers, including the Bedlington, is 12 to 14 years. Of course, some may die at the age of 6 or 8 from cancer or copper toxicosis, or some other life-threatening disease.

GETTING OLD

The bottom line is simply that your dog is getting old when YOU think he is getting old because he slows down in his level of general activity, including walking, running, eating, jumping and retrieving. On the other hand, the frequency of certain activities increases, such as more sleeping, more barking and more repetition of habits like going to the door without being called when you put your coat on to leave the house.

Although the Bedlington matures as early as 14 months of age, dogs generally are considered physically mature at 3 years of age, and can reproduce even earlier. So the first three years of a dog's life are like seven times that of comparable humans. That means a 3-year-old dog is like a 21-year-old human. As the curve of comparison shows, there is no hard and fast rule for comparing dog and human ages. Small breeds tend to live longer than large breeds, some breeds' adolescent periods last longer than others' and some breeds experience rapid periods of growth. The comparison is made even more difficult, for, likewise, not all humans age at the same rate...and human females live longer than human males.

WHAT TO LOOK FOR IN SENIORS

Most veterinary surgeons and behaviourists use the seven-year mark as the time to consider a dog a 'senior.' The term 'senior' does not imply that the dog is geriatric and has begun to fail in mind and body. Ageing is essentially a slowing process. Humans readily admit that they feel a difference in their activity level from age 20 to 30, and then from 30 to 40, etc. By treating the seven-year-old dog as a senior, owners are able to implement certain therapeutic and preventative medical strategies with the help of their veterinary

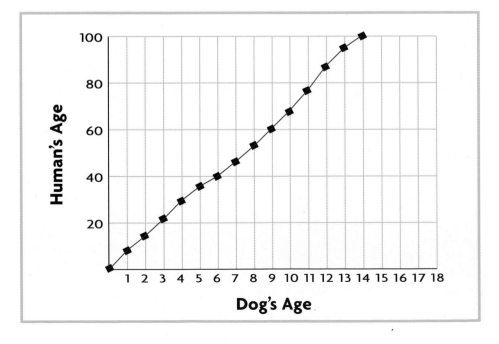

CDS: COGNITIVE DYSFUNCTION SYNDROME
'OLD-DOG SYNDROME'

There are many ways to evaluate old-dog syndrome. Veterinary surgeons have defined CDS (cognitive dysfunction syndrome) as the gradual deterioration of cognitive abilities. These are indicated by changes in the dog's behaviour. When a dog changes its routine response, and maladies have been eliminated as the cause of these behavioural changes, then CDS is the usual diagnosis.

More than half the dogs over eight years old suffer from some form of CDS. The older the dog, the more chance it has of suffering from CDS. In humans, doctors often dismiss the CDS behavioural changes as part of 'winding down.'

There are four major signs of CDS: the dog has frequent toilet accidents inside the home, sleeps much more or much less than normal, acts confused and fails to respond to social stimuli.

SYMPTOMS OF CDS

FREQUENT TOILET ACCIDENTS
- *Urinates in the house.*
- *Defecates in the house.*
- *Doesn't signal that he wants to go out.*

SLEEP PATTERNS
- *Moves much more slowly.*
- *Sleeps more than normal during the day.*
- *Sleeps less during the night.*

CONFUSION
- *Goes outside and just stands there.*
- *Appears confused with a faraway look in his eyes.*
- *Hides more often.*
- *Doesn't recognise friends.*
- *Doesn't come when called.*
- *Walks around listlessly and without a destination.*

FAILS TO RESPOND TO SOCIAL STIMULI
- *Comes to people less frequently, whether called or not.*
- *Doesn't tolerate petting for more than a short time.*
- *Doesn't come to the door when you return home.*

surgeons. A senior-care programme should include at least two veterinary visits per year and screening sessions to determine the dog's health status, as well as nutritional counselling. Veterinary surgeons determine the senior dog's health status through a blood smear for a complete blood count, serum chemistry profile with electrolytes, urinalysis, blood pressure check, electrocardiogram, ocular tonometry (pressure on the eyeball) and dental prophylaxis.

Such an extensive programme for senior dogs is well advised before owners start to see the obvious physical signs of ageing, such as slower and inhibited movement, greying, increased sleep/nap periods and disinterest in play and other activity. This preventative programme promises a longer, healthier life for the ageing dog.

Among the physical problems common in ageing dogs are the loss of sight and hearing, arthritis, kidney and liver failure, diabetes mellitus, heart disease and Cushing's disease (a hormonal disease).

In addition to the physical manifestations discussed, there are some behavioural changes and problems related to ageing dogs. Dogs suffering from hearing or vision loss, dental discomfort or arthritis can become aggressive. Likewise, the near-deaf and/or blind dog may be startled more easily and react in an unexpectedly aggressive manner. Seniors suffering from senility can become more impatient and irritable. Housesoiling accidents are associated with loss of mobility, kidney problems and loss of sphincter control as well as plaque accumulation, physiological brain changes and reactions to medications. Older dogs, just like young puppies, suffer from separation

Old-timers may be more sensitive to heat or cold. A doggie sweater can help ward off the chill in cooler weather.

anxiety, which can lead to excessive barking, whining, housesoiling and destructive behaviour. Seniors may become fearful of everyday sounds, such as vacuum cleaners, heaters, thunder and passing traffic. Some dogs have difficulty sleeping, due to discomfort, the need for frequent toilet visits and the like.

Owners should avoid spoiling the older dog with too many fatty treats. Obesity is a common problem in older dogs and subtracts years from their lives. Keep the senior dog as trim as possible, since excessive weight puts additional stress on the body's vital organs. Some breeders recommend supplementing the diet with foods high in fibre and lower in calories. Adding fresh vegetables and marrow broth to the senior's diet makes a tasty, low-calorie, low-fat supplement. Vets also offer speciality diets for senior dogs that are worth exploring.

Your dog, as he nears his twilight years, needs your patience and good care more than ever. Never punish an older dog for an accident or abnormal behaviour. For all the years of love, protection and companionship that your dog has provided, he deserves special attention and courtesies. The older dog may need to relieve himself at 3 a.m. because he can no longer hold it for eight hours. Older dogs may

EUTHANASIA
Euthanasia must be performed by a licensed veterinary surgeon. There also may be societies for the prevention of cruelty to animals in your area. They often offer this service upon a vet's recommendation.

not be able to remain crated for more than two or three hours. It may be time to give up a sofa or chair to your old friend. Although he may not seem as enthusiastic about your attention and petting, he does appreciate the considerations you offer as he gets older.

Your Bedlington Terrier does not understand why his world is slowing down. Owners must make their dogs' transition into their golden years as pleasant and rewarding as possible.

WHAT TO DO WHEN THE TIME COMES
You are never fully prepared to make a rational decision about putting your dog to sleep. It is very obvious that you love your Bedlington Terrier or you would not be reading this book. Putting a beloved dog to sleep is extremely difficult. It is a decision that must be made with your veterinary surgeon. You are usually forced to make the decision when your dog experiences one or more life-

Cremation is an option for those who wish to memorialise their deceased pets. Cemeteries usually have areas in which to accommodate urns that contain the dogs' ashes.

threatening symptoms that have become serious enough for you to seek medical (veterinary) help.

If the prognosis of the malady indicates that the end is near and that your beloved pet will only continue to suffer and experience no enjoyment for the balance of its life, then euthanasia is the right choice.

WHAT IS EUTHANASIA?

Euthanasia derives from the Greek, meaning *good death*. In other words, it means the planned, painless killing of a dog suffering from a painful, incurable condition, or who is so aged that it cannot walk, see, eat or control its excretory functions. Euthanasia is usually accomplished by injection with an overdose of anaesthesia or a barbiturate. Aside from the prick of the needle, the experience is usually painless.

MAKING THE DECISION

The decision to euthanise your dog is never easy. The days during which the dog becomes ill and the end occurs can be unusually stressful for you. If this is your first experience with the death of a loved one, you may need the comfort dictated by your religious beliefs. If you are the head of the family and have children, you should have involved them in the decision of putting your Bedlington Terrier to sleep. Usually your dog can be maintained on drugs for a few days in order to give you ample time to make a decision. During this time, talking with members of your family or with people who have lived through the same experience can ease the burden of your inevitable decision.

THE FINAL RESTING PLACE

Dogs can have some of the same privileges as humans. The

COPING WITH LOSS

When your dog dies, you may be as upset as when a human companion passes away. You are losing your protector, your baby, your confidante and your best friend. Many people experience not only grief but also feelings of guilt and doubt as to whether they did all that they could for their pet. Allow yourself to grieve and mourn, and seek help from friends and support groups. You may also wish to consult books and websites that deal with this topic.

remains of your beloved dog can be buried in a pet cemetery, which is generally expensive. Dogs who have died at home can be buried in your garden in a place suitably marked with some stone or newly planted tree or bush. Alternatively, your dog can be cremated individually and the ashes returned to you. A less expensive option is mass cremation, although, of course, the ashes cannot then be returned. Vets can usually arrange the cremation on your behalf. The cost of these options should always be discussed frankly and openly with your veterinary surgeon. In Britain, if your dog has died at the surgery, the vet legally cannot allow you to take your dog's body home.

GETTING ANOTHER DOG?

The grief of losing your beloved dog will be as lasting as the grief of losing a human friend or relative. In most cases, if your dog died of old age (if there is such a thing), it had slowed down considerably. Do you want a new Bedlington Terrier puppy to replace it? Or are you better off finding a more mature Bedlington Terrier, say two to three years of age, which will usually be house-trained and will have an already developed personality. In this case, you can find out if you like each other after a few hours of being together.

The decision is, of course, your own. Do you want another Bedlington Terrier or perhaps a different breed so as to avoid comparison with your beloved friend? Most people usually buy the same breed because they know (and love) the characteristics of that breed. Then, too, they often know people who have the same breed and perhaps they are lucky enough that one of their friends expects a litter soon. What could be better?

There are cemeteries for deceased pets. Consult with your veterinary surgeon to help find one in your area.

When you purchase your Bedlington Terrier, you will make it clear to the breeder whether you want one just as a loveable companion and pet, or if you hope to be buying an Bedlington Terrier with show prospects. No reputable breeder will sell you a young puppy and tell you that it is *definitely* of show quality, for so much can go wrong during the early months of a puppy's development. If you plan to show, what you will hopefully have acquired is a puppy with 'show potential.'

To the novice, exhibiting an Bedlington Terrier in the show ring may look easy, but it takes a lot of hard work and devotion to do top winning at a show such as the prestigious Crufts Dog Show, not to mention a little luck too!

The first concept that the canine novice learns when watching a dog show is that each dog first competes against members of its own breed. Once the judge has selected the best member of each breed (Best of Breed), provided that the show is judged on a Group system, that chosen dog will compete with

WINNING THE TICKET
Earning a championship at Kennel Club shows is the most difficult in the world. Compared to the United States and Canada, where it is relatively not 'challenging,' collecting three green tickets not only requires much time and effort, it can be very expensive! Challenge Certificates, as the tickets are properly known, are the building blocks of champions—good breeding, good handling, good training and good luck!

other dogs in its group. Finally, the best of each group will compete for Best in Show and Reserve Best in Show.

The second concept that you must understand is that the dogs are not actually compared against one another. The judge compares each dog against its breed standard, which is a written description of the ideal specimen of the breed. While some early breed standards were indeed based on specific dogs that were famous or popular, many dedicated enthusiasts say that a

SHOW RING ETIQUETTE

Just as with anything else, there is a certain etiquette to the show ring that can only be learned through experience. Showing your dog can be quite intimidating to you as a novice when it seems as if everyone else knows what they are doing. You can familiarise yourself with ring procedure beforehand by taking a class to prepare you and your dog for conformation showing or by talking with an experienced handler. When you are in the ring, listen and pay attention to the judge and follow his/her directions. Remember, even the most skilled handlers had to start somewhere. Keep it up and you too will become a proficient handler before too long!

perfect specimen, as described in the standard, has never walked into a show ring, has never been bred and, to the woe of dog breeders around the globe, does not exist. Breeders attempt to get as close to this ideal as possible with every litter, but theoretically the 'perfect' dog is so elusive that it is impossible. (And if the 'perfect' dog were born, breeders and judges would never agree that it was indeed 'perfect.')

If you are interested in exploring the world of dog showing, your best bet is to join your local breed club. These clubs often host both Championship and Open Shows, and sometimes Match meetings and special events, all of which could be of interest, even if you are only an onlooker. Clubs also send out newsletters, and some organise

A Bedlington Terrier won the Terrier Group at the 2000 Westminster Kennel Club show in the United States.

INFORMATION ON CLUBS

You can get information about dog shows from kennel clubs and breed clubs:

Fédération Cynologique Internationale
14, rue Leopold II, B-6530 Thuin, Belgium
www.fci.be

The Kennel Club
1-5 Clarges St., Piccadilly, London W1Y 8AB, UK
www.the-kennel-club.org.uk

American Kennel Club
5580 Centerview Dr., Raleigh, NC 27606-3390 USA
www.akc.org

Canadian Kennel Club
89 Skyway Ave., Suite 100, Etobicoke, Ontario
M9W 6R4 Canada
www.ckc.ca

training days and seminars in order that people may learn more about their chosen breed. To locate the breed club closest to you, contact The Kennel Club, the ruling body for the British dog world. The Kennel Club governs not only conformation shows but also working trials, obedience shows, agility trials and field trials. The Kennel Club furnishes the rules and regulations for all of these events plus general dog registration and other basic requirements of dog ownership. Its annual show, called the Crufts Dog Show, held in Birmingham, is the largest benched show in England. Every year over 20,000 of the UK's best dogs qualify to participate in this marvellous show, which lasts four days.

The Kennel Club governs many different kinds of shows in Great Britain, Australia, South Africa and beyond. At the most competitive and prestigious of these shows, the Championship Shows, a dog can earn Challenge Certificates (CCs), and thereby become a Show Champion or a Champion. A dog must earn three Challenge Certificates under three different judges to earn the prefix of 'Sh Ch' or 'Ch.' Some breeds must also qualify in a field trial in order to gain the title of full Champion. Challenge Certificates are awarded to a very small percentage of the dogs competing, and dogs that are already Champions compete with others for these coveted CCs. The number of Challenge Certificates awarded in any one year is based upon the total number of dogs in each breed entered for competition.

SEVEN GROUPS

The Kennel Club divides its dogs into seven Groups: Gundog, Utility, Working, Toy, Terrier, Hound and Pastoral.*

*The Pastoral Group, established in 1999, includes those sheepdog breeds previously categorised in the Working Group.

HOW TO ENTER A DOG SHOW
1. Obtain an entry form and show schedule from the Show Secretary.
2. Select the classes that you want to enter and complete the entry form.
3. Transfer your dog into your name at The Kennel Club. (Be sure that this matter is handled before entering.)
4. Find out how far in advance show entries must be made. Oftentimes it's more than a couple of months.

There are three types of Championship Shows: an all-breed General Championship Show for all Kennel-Club-recognised breeds; a Group Championship Show, which is limited to breeds within one of the groups; and a Breed Show, which is usually confined to a single breed. The Kennel Club determines which breeds at which Championship Shows will have the opportunity to earn Challenge Certificates (or tickets). Serious exhibitors often will opt not to participate if the tickets are withheld at a particular show. This policy makes earning championships even more difficult to accomplish.

Open Shows are generally less competitive and are frequently used as 'practice shows' for young dogs. There are hundreds of Open Shows each year that can be delightful social events and are great first show experiences for the novice. Even if you're considering just watching a show to wet your paws, an Open Show is a great choice.

While Championship and Open Shows are most important for the beginner to understand, there are other types of shows in which the interested dog owner can participate. Training clubs sponsor Matches that can be entered on the day of the show for a nominal fee. In these introductory-level exhibitions, two dogs' names are pulled out of a hat and 'matched,' the winner of that match goes on to the next round

For young people interested in showing, junior handling is a wonderful way to learn the ropes. Here, a junior handler and his Bedlington compete in the UK.

CLASSES AT DOG SHOWS

There can be as many as 18 classes per sex for your breed. Check the show schedule carefully to make sure that you have entered your dog in the appropriate class. The classes offered can include Minor Puppy (ages 6 to 9 months), Puppy (ages 6 to 12 months), Junior (ages 6 to 18 months) and Beginners (handler or dog never won first place), as well as the following, each of which is defined in the schedule: Maiden; Novice; Tyro; Debutant; Undergraduate; Graduate; Postgraduate; Minor Limit; Mid Limit; Limit; Open; Veteran; Stud Dog; Brood Bitch; Progeny; Brace and Team.

and eventually only one dog is left undefeated.

Exemption Shows are much more light-hearted affairs with usually only four pedigree classes and several 'fun' classes, all of which can be entered on the day of the show. Exemption Shows are sometimes held in conjunction with small agricultural shows and the proceeds must be given to a charity. Limited Shows are also available in small number. Entry is restricted to members of the club that hosts the show, although one can usually join the club when making an entry.

Before you actually step into the ring, you would be well advised to sit back and observe the judge's ring procedure. If it is your first time in the ring, do not

PRACTISE AT HOME

If you have decided to show your dog, you must train him to gait around the ring by your side at the correct pace and pattern, and to tolerate being handled and examined by the judge. Most breeds require complete dentition, all breeds require a particular bite (scissor, level or undershot) and all males must have two apparently normal testicles fully descended into the scrotum. Enlist family and friends to hold mock trials in your garden to prepare your future champion!

NO SHOW

Never show a dog that is sick, lame or recovering from surgery or infection. Not only will this put your own dog under a tremendous amount of stress, but you will also put other dogs at risk of contracting any illness your dog has. Likewise, bitches who are in heat will distract and disrupt the performances of males who are competing, and bitches that are pregnant will likely be stressed and exhausted by a long day of showing.

Here, the judge evaluates a Bedlington Terrier on a raised table. With small dogs, a table is often used so that the judges can examine the dogs more easily.

be over-anxious and run to the front of the line. It is much better to stand back and study how the exhibitor in front of you is performing. The judge asks each handler to 'stand' the dog, hopefully showing the dog off to his best advantage. The judge will observe the dog from a distance and from different angles, and approach the dog to check his teeth, overall structure, alertness, coat quality and muscle tone, as well as consider how well the dog 'conforms' to the standard. Most importantly, the judge will have the exhibitor move the dog around the ring in some pattern that he or she should specify (another advantage to not going first, but always listen since some judges change their directions—and the judge is always right!). Finally, the judge will give the

dog one last look before moving on to the next exhibitor.

If you are not in the top three at your first show, do not be discouraged. Be patient and consistent, and you may eventually find

A GENTLEMAN'S SPORT

Whether or not your dog wins top honours, showing is a pleasant social event. Sometimes, one may meet a troublemaker or nasty exhibitor, but these people should be ignored and forgotten. In the extremely rare case that someone threatens or harasses you or your dog, you can lodge a complaint with The Kennel Club. This should be done with extreme prudence. Complaints are investigated seriously and should never be filed on a whim.

yourself in the winning line-up. Remember that the winners were once in your shoes and have devoted many hours and much money to earn the placement. If you find that your dog is losing every time and never getting a nod, it may be time to consider a different dog sport or to just enjoy your Bedlington Terrier as a pet.

Virtually all countries with a recognised speciality breed club (sometimes called a 'parent' club) offer show conformation competition specifically for and among Bedlington Terriers. Under direction of the club, other

TEMPERAMENT PLUS
Although it seems that physical conformation is the only factor considered in the show ring, temperament is also of utmost importance. An aggressive or fearful dog should not be shown, as bad behaviour will not be tolerated and may pose a threat to the judge, other exhibitors, you and your dog.

special events for hunting, tracking, obedience and agility may be offered as well, whether for titling or just for fun.

The judge looks over the line-up side-by-side to decide which of the Bedlingtons best conforms to the breed standard.

WORKING TRIALS

Working trials can be entered by any well-trained dog of any breed, not just Gundogs or Working dogs. Many dogs that earn the Kennel Club Good Citizen Dog award choose to participate in a working trial. There are five stakes at both Open and Championship levels: Companion Dog (CD), Utility Dog (UD), Working Dog (WD), Tracking Dog (TD) and Patrol Dog (PD). As in conformation shows, dogs compete against a standard and, if the dog reaches the qualifying mark, it obtains a certificate. The exercises are divided into groups, and the dog must achieve at least 70 percent of the allotted score for each exercise in order to qualify. If the dog achieves 80 percent in the Open level, it receives a Certificate of Merit (COM); in the

TIDINESS COUNTS

Surely you've spent hours grooming your dog to perfection for the show ring, but don't forget about yourself! While the dog should be the centre of attention, it is important that you also appear clean and tidy. Wear smart, appropriate clothes and comfortable shoes in a colour that contrasts with your dog's coat. Look and act like a professional.

THE TITLE OF CHAMPION

Until 1950, a dog in Britain could earn the title of Champion by winning three Challenge Certificates. Today, the prestigious title of Champion requires that the dog win three tickets and qualify in the field. The Kennel Club introduced the title of Show Champion for the dog winning three tickets (but without a field qualification). A Dual Champion is a dog that has obtained the title of Show Champion as well as that of Field Trial Champion.

Championship level, it receives a Qualifying Certificate. At the CD stake, dogs must participate in four groups: Control, Stay, Agility and Search (Retrieve and Nosework). At the next three

SHOW QUALITY SHOWS

While you may purchase a puppy in the hope of having a successful career in the show ring, it is impossible to tell, at eight to ten weeks of age, whether your dog will be a contender. Some promising pups end up with minor to serious faults that prevent them from taking home a Best of Breed award, but this certainly does not mean they can't be the best of companions for you and your family. To find out if your potential show dog is show quality, enter him in a match to see how a judge evaluates him. You may also take him back to your breeder as he matures to see what he might advise.

levels, UD, WD and TD, there are only three groups: Control, Agility and Nosework.

The Agility exercises consist of three jumps: a vertical scale up a wall of planks; a clear jump over a basic hurdle with a removable top bar; and a long jump across angled planks.

To earn the UD, WD and TD, dogs must track approximately one-half mile for articles laid from one-half hour to three hours previously. Tracks consist of turns and legs, and fresh ground is used for each participant. The fifth stake, PD, involves teaching manwork, which is not recommended for this breed.

AGILITY TRIALS

Agility trials began in the United Kingdom in 1977 and have since spread around the world, especially to the United States, where they are very popular. The handler directs his dog over an obstacle course that includes jumps (such as those used in the

'PET PASSPORT'

In the near future we are likely to see dogs from several different countries competing with each other in the same ring. The 'Pet Passport' been brought in, and dogs can now travel abroad without having to go into quarantine upon their return to Britain.

The Bedlington's natural athleticism shows as he flies through a tyre jump at an agility trial.

Dog shows are social events as well, as everyone has one thing in common—a love of his breed. A group of exhibitors chat ringside as they await their turn with their Bedlingtons.

working trials), as well as tyres, the dog walk, weave poles, pipe tunnels, collapsed tunnels, etc. The Kennel Club requires that dogs not be trained for agility until they are 12 months old. This dog sport is great fun for dog and owner, and interested owners should join a training club that has obstacles and experienced agility handlers who can introduce you and your dog to the 'ropes' (and tyres, tunnels, etc.).

FÉDÉRATION CYNOLOGIQUE INTERNATIONALE

Established in 1911, the Fédération Cynologique Internationale (FCI) represents the 'world kennel club.' This international body brings uniformity to

the breeding, judging and showing of pure-bred dogs. Although the FCI originally included only five European nations: France, Germany, Austria, the Netherlands and Belgium (which remains its headquarters), the organisation today embraces nations on six continents and recognises well over 300 breeds of pure-bred dog.

There are three titles attainable through the FCI: the International Champion, which is the most prestigious; the International Beauty Champion, which is based on aptitude certificates in different countries; and the International Trial Champion, which is based on achievement in obedience trials in different countries. Dogs from every country can participate in these impressive canine spectacles, the largest of which is the World Dog Show, hosted in a different country each year. FCI sponsors both national and international shows. The hosting country determines the judging system and breed standards are always based on the breed's country of origin.

The top award in an FCI show is Champion and to gain this title, a dog must win three CACs (*Certificat d'Aptitude au Championnat*) at regional or club shows under three different judges who are breed specialists. The title of International

The Bedlington's abilities give him the potential to star in agility competition. Agility is a 'thinking' sport...plus, it's a great outlet for that terrier energy!

Champion is gained by winning four CACIBs (*Certificat d'Aptitude au Championnat International de Beauté*), which are offered only at international shows, with at least a one-year lapse between the first and fourth award.

The FCI is divided into ten 'Groups.' At the World Dog Show, the following 'Classes' are offered for each breed: Puppy Class (6–9 months), Youth Class (9–18 months), Open Class (15 months or older) and Champion Class. A dog can be awarded a classification of Excellent, Very Good, Good, Sufficient and Not

Sufficient. Puppies can be awarded classifications of Very Promising, Promising or Not Promising. Four placements are made in each class. After all sexes and classes are judged, a Best of Breed is selected. Other special groups and classes may also be shown. Each exhibitor showing a dog receives a written evaluation from the judge.

Besides the World Dog Show and other all-breed shows, you can exhibit your dog at speciality shows held by different breed clubs. Speciality shows may have their own regulations.

INDEX

*Page numbers in **boldface** indicate illustrations.*

My Bedlington Terrier

PUT YOUR PUPPY'S FIRST PICTURE HERE

Dog's Name _____

Date _____ Photographer _____